F O X S P I R I T
A Woman in Mao's China

To Kathleen

張戎文

Mar. 2008

Foxspirit

A popular character in Chinese legend, the fox spirit is a symbol of good and evil, of luck and ill-omen. Disguised as humans, fox spirits often assume the form of women — charming, witty, and manipulative. Calling a woman a fox spirit has a very negative connotation — a woman who seduces and entraps men. Zhimei Zhang was attacked as a fox spirit by some during China's Cultural Revolution.

The true character of the fox spirit is often concealed and distorted in China's male-dominated culture. The fox spirit is a rebel at heart, using her charm and wit to navigate the intricate pathways of a tightly-controlled society and to remain true to herself.

China

FOXSPIRIT
A Woman in Mao's China

Zhimei Zhang

Véhicule Press

EDITED FOR THE PRESS BY KELLY HAGGART
Published with the assistance of The Canada Council.

Cover design: J.W. Stewart
Book design: ECW Type & Art
Printing: Imprimerie d'Édition Marquis Ltée

CANADIAN CATALOGUING IN PUBLICATION DATA

Zhang, Zhimei
  Foxspirit : a woman in Mao's China

ISBN 1-55065-025-4

  1. Zhang, Zhimei. 2. China — Social life and customs — 1949- .
3. China — History — 20th century. 4. Women — China — Biography.
1. Title.

DS778.Z48A3 1992   951.05´092   C92-090427-0

Véhicule Press, P.O.B. 125, Place du Parc Station, Montreal,
Quebec H2W 2M9.

Distributed in Canada by General Distribution Services, 30 Lesmill Road,
Don Mills, Ontario M3B 2T6 and in the United States by Inland Book
Company (East Haven, CT).

Printed in Canada on acid-free paper.

Acknowledgements

I would like to thank all my friends who have given me enormous support since I arrived in Canada. Without them, today's accomplishments would not have been possible. Words cannot express what I owe them.

I wish to express my profound gratitude to my editor and friend Kelly Haggart. I was fortunate to have an editor who has worked in China and knows China. Considering Kelly's significant efforts, I would like to call it *our* book rather than *my* book.

My gratitude also goes to CBC journalist Jon Kalina who showed interest in my manuscript and introduced me to Véhicule Press. Without Jon, this book would have been delayed for an indefinite length of time in search of a publisher.

I owe heartfelt thanks to my friends who read preliminary drafts of the manuscript; their constructive comments helped improve the work.

I thank my sisters for providing me with detailed information on our family history and my two daughters Luna and Yannie who gave me their unqualified support. Without their encouragement, I would not have been able to complete this project.

Financial assistance from The Canada Council Explorations program and the Multiculturalism program of the Secretary of State gave me the time to make *Foxspirit* a reality. Credit must also go to Patrick Watson, George Bain, Mark Abley, Yves Sanssouci, and Jean Duval who generously provided letters of support.

It is time to move from this dream to another.

Table of Contents

Prologue

"The masses have reported that Zhang Zhimei has serious problems. She is hereby ordered to appear at the Dictatorship Group Headquarters at 2:00 p.m. today."

I thought my heart would burst through my chest as I read the words. For the other teachers crowding around the school bulletin board, my detention notice was just one of many such posters that went up in the summer of 1968, the third year of Mao's Cultural Revolution. No one spoke to me as I fought my way out of the throng. I felt numb as I walked home across the campus.

My husband, Pang, was waiting for me. He had already seen the poster. "I'll pack for you," he said gently. "Don't try to resist. But try not to be too scared. I have ways of finding out how you're being treated."

We set off before the deadline, Pang carrying my bedroll. We had been married only three months.

"Don't look so depressed," he said. "We don't have to look completely downtrodden, you know." And so we tried to smile and hold our heads high as we crossed the campus.

Students shouted out when they saw us: "Look at him! He's smiling. Hey, Pang! Proud of her, are you?" "He's even carrying her things for her!" "Don't either of you have any sense of shame?"

Keep your head up, I kept reminding myself. I felt sorrier for

Pang than for myself. I was already in disgrace and had little left to lose, but why did he have to share this humiliation? My accusers said that I was an immoral woman. And, because of letters exchanged with an East German friend, I was suspected of being a spy.

One of my former students was waiting for me at the Dictatorship Group Headquarters. I used to give Hao special coaching because he had a speech impediment. Now he avoided meeting my eyes as he showed me to my cell.

"Put her things here," he said to Pang. "And you leave now."

The room was just big enough for a narrow cot. The windowpane had been painted black, but light filtered through a strip left bare at the top.

"I have to look through your things," Hao said. "It's the rule." Everything passed inspection except a small pair of scissors in my sewing-kit.

"You can't have those. It's unsafe," he said.

Don't worry, kid, I thought. I'm not going to kill myself.

At nightfall, locked in my cell, still feeling dazed, I undressed and turned off the light. It felt so strange to be doing these ordinary things in such an extraordinary situation. Just a few months earlier, I had thought I had some sort of future. Now my whole world had collapsed.

As I was about to lie down, a voice on the other side of the door shouted: "Keep the light on!" I noticed the hole in the door through which the guard peeped from time to time.

"I can't sleep with the light on," I said.

"That's not my problem," he said. "It's the rule. If you can't sleep, use the time to think about what you'll write in your confession."

I switched the light back on, turned my face to the wall and wept as soundlessly as possible. I got no sleep that night. The next night I made a lampshade out of an issue of the People's Daily to cover the bare lightbulb and did manage to sleep.

The months of solitude ahead would allow me plenty of time to think, to review my past and brood on the future. I had tried hard to fit into the accepted mold, to smooth my rough edges, to confess my innermost thoughts, to do things that went against my conscience and my personality to demonstrate my loyalty to the system. What had I gained? I was still an outcast in my own culture: a divorced woman, who had foreign friends and a "bad" family background. I would never be accepted, and my children would also bear the stigma. It had taken me 20 years of adult life to realize this.

After I was detained, Pang came under enormous pressure from teachers in the "revolutionary" camp to join the attack on me. To one, who suggested he save his own skin by doing so, he said: "To call Zhimei a spy is practically a compliment. Unfortunately, she doesn't have the head for spying. If she's a spy, then everyone in China is a spy."

Pang now tried to stay away from everyone, even his closest friends. He knew that normal human relations, that friendships, no longer existed. "My policy," he said, "was not to trust anybody at all at that point."

One evening while he was home cooking his dinner, Zhu appeared. Once his roommate and close friend, Zhu had been sent by the revolutionary teachers to find out what Pang was thinking. He was careful not to say anything much to his old friend. But while Pang was busy preparing his meal, Zhu picked up a small black book lying on the table. It was an address book of mine that went back years, containing the addresses and phone numbers of people I had known when I worked for the Ministry of Foreign Trade in the 1950s. It held the names of the East European commercial attachés I had called regularly on business as well as the names of colleagues who took part in the ministry's annual ping-pong tournament.

As Zhu leafed through the book, he became convinced he had made a great discovery. Here were lots of names, any of which might be an important clue. As a bonus, some of the names were foreign. Zhu must have been delirious as he sprinted to the Dictatorship Group to report his find. The next day, Pang was ordered to hand over "the black book."

That day, I received a new order: write down the names of everybody I had ever known, even going back to early childhood friends. I was to detail my relationship with each of them, the place and date we met, how long we had kept in touch and everything we did together during the period of our acquaintance. It was an impossible task, but I made a stab at it.

A few days later, I was summoned to the interrogation room, where a group of revolutionary teachers had been assembled. As usual, I sat in the middle of the semi-circle as they grilled me about my relationship with dozens of people. Many of the names mentioned were foreign and unfamiliar. They were not on the list I had been ordered to draw up of everyone I had known. I also didn't recognize many of the Chinese names being lobbed at me. I was confused, unable to figure out what they were after.

"It seems you won't co-operate," one of the teachers said after several hours of fruitless cross-examination, "and so we'll have to 'keep company' with you until you do."

"Keeping company" was the Dictatorship Group's latest innovation. Victims were made to stand for hours until, exhausted, they were ready to confess to anything. I stood the whole night during a non-stop interrogation, while the inquisition team, my fellow teachers, changed every three hours.

"Tell me, Comrade Zhang . . . . " Gao, one of my interrogators, hesitated, realizing his slip of the tongue.

Zhu, Pang's former friend, snapped: "You can't call her comrade!"

"Down with Zhang Zhimei!" Gao shouted, correcting his tone.

"What is your relationship with Yuri Melamed? With Zinovy Dovlatov? With Helmut Mohr? Speak up!" Zhu howled.

I lifted my head wearily and looked at him out of the corner of my eye. Zhu, you bastard, I thought in disgust. What right have you to make these insinuations? I think we both remember how you asked to use my room when you wanted to be alone with your lover, a married woman. I locked the two of you in from the outside, to avoid raising suspicion – remember?

"Down with the international woman hooligan Zhang Zhimei!" came another voice. I could hardly believe my ears. But I didn't have to look up; I knew it was my old friend Lin. We had spent long hours together in the past, talking like sisters. I didn't know exactly what she meant by "international woman hooligan," but it sounded humiliating enough.

My dear friend, I thought, the days I spent encouraging you to be strong and to make a fresh start seem like yesterday. You were so depressed when you came to our school. If it hadn't been for that love affair, you would have been assigned to the Foreign Ministry. The man didn't miss a beat – he went on to greater things – but the affair ruined your career. I held you as you wept.

By daybreak, my feet were swollen from standing, my hands puffy from hanging down all night. I was exhausted, but they got nothing out of me. There was nothing to get.

After I was released, I learned that my little black address book had been the cause of all the excitement. The names in it were thought to be the spies in my network. No wonder many of the names didn't ring a bell when I was interrogated: they were the amateur ping-pong players in the Ministry of Foreign Trade in the 1950s. For a time I had been tournament organizer and the numbers entered beside names in my book were simply the scores of matches. My interrogators were convinced they were some kind of code.

A friend was subjected to a crueller session. Like me, she had been accused of being a loose woman. At a mass meeting, she was forced to take off her clothes and stand naked before a jeering crowd. The humiliation was too much to bear, and she killed herself soon afterwards.

Even during the darkest days, I never contemplated suicide. I had come to view my accusers at criticism meetings as lousy actors in a bad play. And I wanted to see the end of the play, which, for some reason, I believed would not last long. I never thought of myself as the weak one, because bullying the powerless was never my idea of strength. And I always had faith that some day my fortunes would be reversed. I had no idea how or when that might happen, but I was determined to live to that day.

Chapter One

A REVOLUTIONARY HAIRCUT
AND LIBERATED FEET

My mother was slapping mahjong tiles on to a table around daybreak on June 19, 1935. She had been sitting with her gambling buddies since the previous evening, bulging stomach rubbing uncomfortably against the table's edge whenever she leaned forward to pick up a playing tile.

"More soup!" she called to the amah hovering nearby. The peasant serving woman had little chance of sleep on nights like these. During sessions that might easily last eight to ten hours, she ferried food and drink to the four players hunched over the gaming table. She kept soup simmering for hours on the coal stove; on this night, dates and lotus seeds swam in a sweet broth. My mother was convinced dates were good for the blood because of their reddish colour. Similarly, walnuts were good for the brain because of their shape.

The amah put a bowl of soup on each of four side tables arranged around the mahjong table. A small tray on one of the side tables held the cut of each winning take that went to the amah. Not much went into the tray after each victory, but small sums could add up nicely if the game lasted until dawn.

Now and then she would disappear into the bedroom next door to stoke the opium pipe. Soon a player would slip away to recline on a soft bed against freshly plumped-up pillows, the way a pipe was meant to be smoked. Afterwards, the player would rejoin the game in refreshed good humour.

My mother was thirty-eight, pregnant and a gambling addict. I was her eighth pregnancy and even in its final moments it was causing no great excitement. The contractions began early in the game and grew in intensity, keeping pace with the action. She stayed at the table as long as she could, trying to soothe the pain and stave off the inevitable with warm bowls of soup.

"I was winning!" she told me years later. "Naturally I didn't want to leave."

Wherever my father was that night, he was praying for a son. So far, in almost twenty years of marriage, sons that were born had all died before reaching their teens. When I came along, he already had three daughters and could see no need for another. He was devastated when the hospital nurse brought the bad news. Frustrated but ever hopeful, he named me Zhimei, using written characters that mean "Stop Girl." In time, this command took effect; at forty-two, my mother gave it one last try and produced a son who survived.

The pronunciation of my given name never changed, but the characters used to write it, and hence its meaning, underwent considerable revision over the years. When my father was signing me up for school he suddenly felt ashamed at the name he had given me and on the spot changed the way the second character was written. Thus it came to pass that my name was Stop Girl as I walked with my father to school on my first day, but Stop Beautiful on the way home.

How could you be called Stop Beautiful when you weren't beautiful to begin with? And suppose I was beautiful, why should I stop? Even my father's second inspiration bothered me. Other girls had conventionally pretty names like Elegant Pearl, Radiant Plumage, Delicate Serenity, Fragrant Lotus or Gorgeous Summer. Several years later, without my father's consent, I added a few strokes to the first character in my given name, changing "stop" to "white herb." Beautiful White Herb was a big improvement, I felt, but my father never accepted the change. He was convinced there should be some sense of "stop" in my name and for the rest of his life whenever he wrote me, he wrote to Stop Beautiful.

My mother was very spoiled. She was the pet in a wealthy landlord's family that had more than enough money to lavish on its children. She did embroidery and painting, as did most women of her class. But she also learned to read and write, a rare accomplishment in that era, especially for a small-town girl.

You had only to glance down at her feet to see she was a rebel by nature. She had fought to have her feet unwrapped before they were completely misshapen by the binding cloth. She was left with what are known as "liberated feet," feet that had won a reprieve before being irreversibly tortured down to the "three-inch ideal." Her feet were certainly smaller than they would have been had natural growth occurred, and the big toes permanently overlapped the second toes. But in those feet that were only semi-deformed, anyone of the day could recognize the evidence of a strong will.

My mother loved social exuberance and financial extravagance, and the two came together for her in gambling. She actually did seem to have a bit of luck at mahjong, while my father had neither luck nor interest in his wife's chief compulsion. His passions were calligraphy, music and poetry. In short, my parents had little in common.

"I married her because I felt I owed her family something," my father told me.

"Your father came to our family with nothing," my mother often grumbled. "We fed him, clothed him, gave him money to study in Japan." She felt she had married beneath her, and in their frequent quarrels she never hesitated to bring up his humble origins. When his career began to falter, she reminded him of a fortune-teller's prediction that he would have a "beggar's fate" because of the shape of his nose. Fat and flat, it lacked the fine silhouette of the noses on men of good fortune, she said. These fights were deeply humiliating for my father and the family was seldom at peace.

Born a month apart in 1897 (the year of the rooster, according to the traditional calendar), my parents were eighteen when they married. Later in life, my mother would say with conviction that women should not marry until thirty-five, that they needed time to develop their real selves before their lives were given over to husband and family. And, after one of the many battles of their married life, she heaved an exasperated sigh and muttered: "A rooster should never marry another rooster, because roosters like to fight."

My parents were both born in Jinxiang, a walled town in the relatively prosperous east-coast province of Zhejiang. Economic prosperity was one reason for the region's higher educational level. Another was that Japan lay just across the water, and many people went there for training not available in China.

Zhejiang produced more than its share of luminaries: China's literary giant Lu Xun was from the canal town of Shaoxing, as was the late premier Zhou Enlai. And not far from Shaoxing, a decade before Zhou's birth, Kuomintang leader Chiang Kai-shek was born in the town of Fenghua.

Four wealthy landowning families lived in Jinxiang: Xia (my mother's surname), Zhang (my father's), Yin and Chen. The Xia and Zhang families got on well together and so my mother and father were betrothed before they were born. It was not uncommon in those days for close friends to arrange a marriage between their offspring while the pair were still slumbering in the womb. This custom is called "point at the belly and arrange a marriage."

There were ways to guess the sex of the fetus which did seem to be accurate more often than not. If a woman's belly protruded straight out, chances were it was a boy; if it was more spread out to the sides, it was a girl. People also took note of the food a woman craved early in the pregnancy: a taste for sour things meant it was a girl; spicy, and it was a boy.

Ensuring that the clan's lineage was kept unbroken was as urgent an item of family business as keeping the ancestors' graves swept clean. It would have been considered the utmost irresponsibility to leave marriage to the whim of individuals. Romantic love had no part to play.

Grandfather Zhang, my father's father, was a wealthy scholar and landowner who lived comfortably on his rental incomes. His wife, whom he adored, was pretty and talented. She could read and write and paint. When she and the infant died during her first childbirth, my grandfather sank into depths of despondency from which he never emerged. But not even acute depression kept him from his duty to carry on the family name. He married a woman from the countryside whom he did not love, and she bore him two sons and two daughters. She was very shortsighted, at a time when glasses were only available to an emperor. Pu Yi, the last to occupy the imperial throne, had a pair, but not a small-town woman with poor eyesight. It was small wonder she was illiterate.

Hoping to alleviate his own anguish, Grandfather Zhang turned himself into a philanthropist who responded lavishly to every plea. Word got around, and an endless stream of needy people flowed through the house; the family's wealth flowed out the door with them when they left. Through the generosity which had sprung from his grief, Grandfather Zhang led his own family to ruin. Shame was added to his store of miseries and one day he disappeared down to the river and threw himself off a bridge.

My father was three, and his brother only months old, when their father died. Five years later, their mother died of typhus, casting four orphans into the world. The two girls, not yet teenagers, were married off as child brides. The two sons were sent to the families with whom marriage deals had been struck years before. My father joined my mother's family, and they were siblings for ten years before they were married. Out of respect for Grandfather Zhang's memory as a serious and generous man, my father was treated well by the Xia family. His new parents liked him a lot because of his scholarly qualities: he was literate, timid, reserved.

My mother already had a brother of her own. My uncle was a rebel who dreamed of going to Japan to further his study of revolutionary ideas. He never made it. In 1906 he fell ill with tuberculosis. From his sickbed one day, he asked my mother to bring him a pair of scissors. Then he tore them from her hand, swung them to the back of his head and snipped. My mother looked on in horror: elder brother had cut off his pigtail!

The Manchus who ruled over the ethnic Han majority during the Qing dynasty (1644-1911) ordered their male subjects to shave their heads, leaving only a Manchu-style pigtail. The penalty for flouting this rule was death: a Han kept his hair and lost his head or kept his head and lost his hair. By snipping off his pigtail, my uncle was committing a bold act of defiance against the Qing emperor.

"The revolution has begun!" he screamed, whipping the length of hair violently back and forth. His face was blazing with fever as he lay back, exhausted, against sweat-soaked pillows. Suddenly my mother felt nailed to the wall by his bloodshot eyes. They had snapped open and seemed to be staring, wide and hopeful, into the bright revolutionary future. Not long after his feverish, unfilial act, he was dead. Grandfather Xia was a broken man. He went around showing his son's queue to people, saying sadly: "My son has cut short his life and gone to make revolution."

The words and deeds of a dying man were treated with special respect. Even the outrageous demands of a revolutionary might be heeded after his death, as they never were in life. Uncle's last words were about my mother: "Leave sister's feet unbound. And send her to school."

Indeed, he had been the first to encourage my mother to unwind the binding cloth from around her feet. He did it for her himself the first time, tenderly unwrapping the pinched feet and then concealing the cloth beneath layers of garbage in a bin. At first she was tearfully compliant when my grandmother insisted on rebinding her feet. Later, emboldened by her brother, she argued as passionately as he had that her feet should be given what little chance they had left for normal growth.

My grandparents were not pleased with the situation, but my uncle's death lent new weight to his words and they were forced to relent. They also saw to it that his other dying wish was fulfilled. When a school was set up in town, off my mother went. It was most unusual for a girl to go to school and at first she was the only one in the class among the sons of landlords and merchants. She attended for several years, which is why she learned to read and write and use an abacus.

For this reason, and because her brother had died, my mother functioned as the son in the family. Grandfather Xia, who was getting on, was glad there was someone to take his place and make the rounds collecting the grain the peasants paid as rent. "I should have been born a boy. I would have made a very successful man!" my mother said.

For his part, my father began his formal education in 1906, not long after the imperial examination system was abolished and schools were set up. At eighteen he married, and at nineteen he set off by himself for Japan. His adoptive parents gave him money to make the crossing to Kobe in 1916. He spent his first two years in Japan learning the language and in the third year began a university economics course. After graduation, the Mitsubishi Bank in Tokyo hired him because he could work an abacus and do bookkeeping. "If you do well, you'll be earning the same salary as our Japanese workers after a while," he was told. It was customary in Japan, as elsewhere, to pay Chinese workers less.

My father had been on the job for only two weeks when an earthquake struck Tokyo with deadly force on September 1, 1923. My mother, back in Jinxiang with their two children, heard nothing from him after the quake. She didn't know whether he was dead or alive. After enduring this silence for three months, she decided to go and see for herself.

My parents had lived apart for seven years. My father had come home for only one brief visit, during which a son, Long, was conceived. The boy, now four, had never seen his father. Mei, their daughter, was now seven and she, too, knew her father only from a picture he had sent of himself in a kimono.

"Look at that getup!" a neighbour hooted when Mei showed her the picture. "Looks like your papa's joined a monastery!"

My mother, meanwhile, was worried that her husband's conduct during his years alone was less than monk-like. She had heard a rumour that he had actually married a Japanese woman. If she found him alive when she got to Tokyo, she would demand an immediate explanation. If the rumour turned out not to be true, she was still worried he had grown used to all that freedom and would never return to take care of his family.

Grandfather Xia accompanied his daughter and her two children on the daylong trip up the river to the seaport of Wenzhou, where she and the children boarded a steamship to Kobe. Grandfather was anxious about the whole enterprise and about what ridiculous scene she might stumble upon when she arrived in Japan. He ground his teeth with worry during his trip back home by creaky junk.

My plucky mother headed off serenely into the unknown because she knew she had made careful preparations. She had, for instance, committed to memory three emergency sentences in Japanese. When she had nothing else to think about on board the ship, she bowed her head and moved it gently up and down as she had seen Japanese in China do when they spoke. And while she rocked, she repeated her three sentences over and over. The boat was rocking, my mother was rocking and fellow passengers weaving past could hear her say: "I need a rickshaw. I'm looking for a restaurant. I want to buy food for my children."

When they reached Kobe, she took a rickshaw (that sentence worked!) to a telegraph office where she sent my father a simple cable alerting him to the time of their arrival in Tokyo. If her husband was still living at the address she had for him, if he was still alive, she felt sure he would meet them when they arrived at the Tokyo railway station.

My mother was tired; the train ride was rough. Portions of the track had just been repaired, and evidence of the devastating quake flashed by the window. When they pulled into Tokyo station, she felt sick to her stomach. After scanning the faces on the platform, she felt even sicker. Her worst fear was realized. No husband. He had been flattened in the quake. Perhaps when the earth moved he had been with his Japanese wife and they had both been flattened. She cheered up a little at that. She didn't know what she would do if she got to the place where his home should have been and found a mound of rubble. She headed for the exit, lumbering under the possessions strapped to her back and dragging a tired child with each hand. She hailed a rickshaw and showed the driver the return address written on a tattered envelope.

My mother felt wretched as the driver pulled his load around a corner and on to the street named on the envelope. But then she noticed that the damage seemed to be light in this area. Now one fear replaced another: her heart began to pound as she imagined walking in on her live husband in the embrace of his live Japanese wife. The rickshaw stopped in front of a hostel which, although nothing fancy, was all in one piece. She knocked on my father's door, growing more anxious by the minute about what lay behind it. No answer. She opened the door.

Odour of tobacco. Piles of books and heaps of clothes. Rumpled quilt on tatami sleeping mat. The room was lived in.

Mei and Long stopped sniffling and began exploring. My mother lay down and within minutes succumbed to her exhaustion. Half an hour later the door was flung open and Mei and Long ran to her side, whimpering. Mei shook her mother: "Ma, wake up! There's a man!"

My mother forced her eyes open and saw her husband for the first time in five years. Words came bounding out of her mouth like attack dogs: "Where have you been? Why didn't you meet us?"

My father was equally angry: "I was there! Why didn't you look for me?" It turned out that as my mother was dashing out of the station, my father had been dashing in by another entrance. That first irritated exchange broke the silence of their long separation and set the tone for the rest of their married life.

My mother did not find another woman on the scene, but after badgering a neighbour she learned my father had had company for several years. When that woman, who was Japanese, learned my father had a wife in China, she departed. She did not want to be a concubine. For the rest of his life, my father kept a picture of an attractive Japanese woman in his photo album and never explained who she was. We suspected it was *her*. Years later, with my parents' loveless marriage filling our home with unhappiness, Mei said she wished our father had married the other woman: "He would have had a better life if he had a wife he had liked."

Chapter Two

THE TURTLES HAVE
THEIR STRAW HATS ON

Some years after the family reunion in Tokyo, a neighbour, watching my older siblings at play with other children, remarked to my father: "Your children are just like Japanese kids now." It was meant as a compliment, but my father didn't take it that way. He decided then and there to return to China. His children could barely speak Chinese any more. He wanted them to grow up knowing who they were.

After the family's return from Japan in 1931, my father found work with the Bank of China in Fengtian, a twelve-hour train ride northeast of Beijing. (In those days Fengtian was known to foreigners as Mukden; after Liberation, it was renamed Shenyang.) Fengtian was the seat of the Japanese puppet government of Manchukuo, set up after Japan occupied northeast China in September 1931. The Japanese installed Pu Yi as monarch of Manchukuo. He had been China's last emperor, toppled when the Qing dynasty fell two decades earlier. It was in the puppet kingdom presided over by Pu Yi that I was born in 1935.

My father had been educated in Japan, but he was still a patriot and in Manchukuo he took the occasional crazy risk to assert this fact. On the "double ten" holiday of October 10, which marked the anniversary of the 1911 founding of the Chinese Republic, my father put up the Kuomintang flag on the roof of the Bank of

China building where he worked. But in those days the only acceptable flags in that area were those of Japan or its puppet government. The Manchukuo authorities called the bank manager and demanded to know the name of the perpetrator. My father confessed when confronted, and the incident was recorded in his file.

I was two when we moved to Beijing (then called Beiping) in early 1937. A friend of my father's from university days had urged him to accept a job with the Construction Ministry. At first he was reluctant; after all, the ministry, like most things in those days, was controlled by the Japanese. Eventually he decided he would be doing the Chinese people no harm in the position being offered to him, which involved overseeing the construction of new roads and bridges in major cities in the north. His fate after Liberation would have been very different had he done a job that had caused harm.

I was too young to understand much about the occupation. If I had lived in the countryside and been forced to witness the acts of real barbarism there, my political education might have been more profound. But there was less overt cruelty in Beijing. I remember seeing Japanese soldiers walking around the city with big swords dangling from their belts; Japanese women with heavily powdered faces moving about in kimonos, children strapped to their backs; Japanese girls roving around in groups wearing their navy blue school uniforms. Strange food and other new things appeared in stores; Japanese signs sprouted all over the city and Japanese was now taught in schools.

Our servants called them "Japanese devils," so I was confused when well-dressed devils came to our home and were treated like guests. My parents taught my sister Wen and me, both born after the family's return from Japan, how to greet the devils in their own language.

We lived in a massive courtyard house in central Beijing, on Arrow Workshop Alley. It had two courtyards, twenty-four rooms, servants' quarters and a garage. In those days, rooms were a standard size, calculated according to the number of pillars. Our living-room, for instance, was a "six-room" hall. It was so huge that even two giant coal stoves going full blast could not keep it warm.

My parents' bedroom was the warmest spot in the house, always kept at a comfortable temperature. But the rooms the children slept in were not heated; my father believed children should be brought up tough. I often couldn't bring myself to climb out of a warm bed in the middle of a winter's night to go to the toilet. My sisters teased me ruthlessly about my bed-wetting and in reply to their taunts, I would burst into tears.

In fact, they called me the "constantly weeping child." I wept when I lost a game, when I couldn't assemble a toy, or when I made a mess of my homework. But I wept most piteously when I got a sore on my tongue, which usually happened after I ate huge quantities of roasted peanuts. Then I would have to hang out my tongue while my mother administered drops of a bitter-tasting traditional medicine. My mother distrusted Western medicine and believed that, given time, the body's immune system would over- come any illness. That approach may help explain the early deaths of some of my siblings.

The first big event after we moved into the mansion was my brother Sheng's "full-month celebration," a traditional party held a month after a child's birth. Sheng, born in 1939, was my parents' last child and only son, so it was a lavish affair. A stage was set up in the front courtyard and musicians performed Peking Opera to an appreciative crowd. I was terrified by the din produced by drums, gongs and cymbals, and stuck my fingers in my ears. I never grew to like Peking Opera any better.

Sheng was dressed in a red silk outfit topped off by a black skullcap. My opinion, at the age of four, was that he looked like he had half a watermelon rind on his head. Guests streamed in and out, each tucking a bright red packet containing new bills of money inside his silk gown. Some also brought tiny ornamental locks made of silver, jade or gold to be hung around his neck for good luck. They were meant to secure a child in the family and keep it from being snatched away by evil or illness.

A few days after the party, Mei, now in her twenties, heard people clambering around on the roof. "Bring me my pistol!" she joked to one of our servants. "I'll fight off these bandits!" It was, in fact, no joke. Two armed men soon forced open the door of her room.

"Hand over your pistol!" one of them yelled. Up on the roof, they had overheard Mei's remark. She managed to convince them she did not really have one.

"We're just passers-by who need some money for travelling expenses," one of the men said as he made menacing gestures with a gun. Mei gave them her jewelry box, but they weren't satisfied with her gold rings and diamond watch. They walked her at gunpoint to the locked door of our parents' bedroom, where both were sleeping. She yelled through the door, in Japanese, that robbers were holding a gun at her back.

My father was trembling as he handed my mother's jewelry box through the door. Along with her valuables, the box contained the tiny locks the family had been given at Sheng's full-month celebration. We suspected that grandiose event had provoked the theft.

The thieves robbed ten other families before they were caught. When my father was summoned by the police to claim the stolen goods, he discovered that the thieves had melted down all the gold they had stolen from the eleven houses into one big lump. It was impossible to tell how much of it was ours and how much belonged to the other victims. He returned home, exasperated. By the time the whole thing was sorted out, he said, we would only have enough gold left to hand over to the police, anyway. They expected a thank-you gift for solving a crime. He let the matter drop and refused to join in the neighbours' wrangling over the lump of gold. It was the last gold our family ever owned.

We went for days without seeing our parents. My father worked late and frequently dined out. I loved it when he was home to tell us stories around the dinner table. My favourites were the ones he told from *Tales of Liaozhai*, by seventeenth century storyteller Pu Songling, about fox spirits. These were foxes that assumed the form of young, beautiful women in order to seduce and entrap men. Other times he would tell us stories about our own family. I was most impressed with his tale of my heaven-sent cousin.

"Not long before the death of your mother's brother, you know, the one who cut off his queue," he began, "a marriage was hastily arranged. The family thought that would banish the evil spirit that had taken up residence in his body. They searched nearby villages and finally found a poor peasant woman who didn't mind marrying a dying man. She was attractive and diligent, but your uncle didn't like her because she had bound feet. He died weeks after the marriage, leaving your aunt a widow. According to custom, she was now obliged to look after a mother-in-law who was a virtual stranger.

Your uncle's death was a real blow to the family, because it had no other son to carry on its name. The women of the family got together to iron out this difficulty. A widow was often not seen in public for several months after bereavement. Your aunt caused no gossip by staying for long stretches inside the high walls of the family compound. When she did go out, she concealed increasingly plump pillows around her middle.

When a woman went into labour, all the elderly members of the family would pull up stools outside the bedroom to wait for the announcement. On the day, the 'virgin birth' was carefully stage-managed. The senior relatives assembled according to normal practice outside the bedroom, in case visitors stopped by with greetings. Before the midwife was called in, an infant boy was delivered – through the front gate, hidden in a decoy shipment of grain. He had been bought that morning from a poor peasant family, along with his afterbirth.

Robbed of the excitement of an actual birth, the women in the family felt there should still be some drama surrounding the baby's arrival. They decided on a complex scenario in which the child would descend from on high, as if a gift from heaven. Sheets were knotted together and the baby was lowered from the attic through a hole in the floor and down on to the curtained four-poster bed on which your aunt lay. The infant swinging in the makeshift hammock officially became part of the family when he touched down on your aunt's belly.

When the midwife came, she was surprised to find the child already born. It had all happened so quickly, the women explained, there had been no time to fetch her beforehand. On proud display was a pan brimming with the afterbirth. Apart from a scrawny, wailing infant, it was the only evidence in the room of the birth. A wet nurse was hired for the peasant boy who, through an accident of fate, had been handed the job of carrying on the family name. He never did learn his true origins and still lives somewhere in Taiwan."

My father would also tell us ghost stories, some of which were so scary that later I would be afraid to go to my bedroom alone: that meant crossing our vast living-room in the pitch dark. A weeping willow outside the window looked like a woman's head, long hair waving in the wind. I would close my eyes, hold my breath and dart into my bedroom, where the slightest creaking of a floorboard terrified me. I shared the room with Wen, who was two years older. But I longed for there to be an adult nearby, someone to cuddle us and read a bedtime story.

Occasionally my father would take us to a park to catch crickets. He would swing his arms back and forth militaristically and we would chorus "one, two, three" as we marched around the park. On the way home, he would buy us croissants from the French bakery. Called "ox horns" because of their shape, they didn't have the rich taste of real croissants because butter was scarce. But we liked them because of their funny shape.

I loved those walks, but they were rare events. We saw even less of our mother. When we left for school, she was still in bed because she had been out all night playing mahjong. When we got home in the afternoon, she was getting ready to leave again.

She was very superstitious and imposed strict rules in the house on the days she played mahjong, which was almost every day. We must never ask her for money before she left for a game. We would sooner ask classmates to lend us what we needed than invite our mother's rage with any unlucky talk of money. To raise the topic of tuition, we would wait until a day when she was in a good mood, which normally meant she had won the night before.

We mentioned the word "shu" (to lose) at our peril. The word was not welcome in our house, in any context. When she was preparing to go out to a game, we were not to mention books. And we were never, ever to sit near her mahjong table reading a book. This prohibition stemmed from the fact that book is also "shu" in Chinese, written with a different character than "to lose" but pronounced the same way.

She never took us on outings. Rainy days were hardest to bear. I felt myself a prisoner, with nowhere to go. But I loved to sit under the eaves in the courtyard and watch as the driving rain created bubbles on the surface of a developing pond. The drainage system was old, and water would stay ankle-deep in the courtyard for hours after a downpour. As rainwater flooded the yard, I would sing to myself: "Raining, raining, cats and dogs; the turtles have their straw hats on." I found this nonsense rhyme, for it does rhyme in Chinese, very amusing.

I liked spending time with the servants. They had interesting stories to tell about their own families in the countryside. Amah Sun, my brother's wet-nurse, was good-looking, good-humoured, smart, neat and efficient. These were the qualities people looked for in a wet-nurse, because it was believed that babies took after the women who nursed them. She made shoes for my dolls, miniature versions of the embroidered silk shoes my mother wore in summer. I adored Amah Sun.

"Do you have children?" I asked her.

"Yes, one son, the same age as our young master," she said.

"But you're always here! Who's looking after him? Don't you miss him?"

"I have to make a living. My husband works in the fields and doesn't earn much. The pay here is good and anyway, our young master here needs me."

"But what does your baby eat? Is there someone to breast-feed him?"

"His grandmother takes care of him. Most of the time she feeds him rice gruel, and occasionally he suckles at the breast of his aunt." I often thought of Amah Sun's own son as she cradled my brother at her breast and wondered if he was receiving the same loving care.

Sometimes I would sneak into the kitchen in search of the servants' food. The cook, a quiet man with a ready smile, made cornbread that was especially good. "Don't let your mother catch you!" he would say with a conspiratorial grin. "Such coarse grain is no good for a young lady's digestion."

I thought there was no neater woman in the world than Amah Li, our housekeeper. Everything about her was spotlessly clean, down to her white socks and black cotton shoes. She was a Manchu from the north; they were known for their politeness and neatness.

I loved to watch her comb her long hair and then sweep it up into a bun. Her hair was like ebony, dark and shiny. She would dip her comb into a gel she concocted from wood shavings soaked in water. It kept her hair healthy, she said.

"Can I use some?" I thought my own long hair would then look as nice as hers without having to wash it, which I loathed.

"Your mother wouldn't like that," she said. "This is not stuff for a proper young lady." The servants were always telling us our mother wouldn't like it if we did things the way they did things, but meanwhile they seemed to be having all the fun.

My childhood was largely confined within the walls of our huge house. My mother didn't like us to play with the neighbours' children, but Wen and I often sneaked into the courtyard next door. The sights and sounds there were too strange not to investigate.

The mother of the Tian family was an obstetrician who had studied in the United States and come back to set up her own maternity hospital. They also had two courtyards; they lived around one and the maternity ward encircled the other. Our mother had declared it off limits, but that didn't stop us crouching in a corner to watch the goings-on: women padding around the courtyard in the last stages of pregnancy; nurses bustling to and fro. We stuffed rags under the dolls' dresses so they would look like the women shuffling around the courtyard. And then we would shriek in agony, as we had heard the women shriek.

Once, screams coming from one of the rooms were more blood-curdling than usual. A nurse came upon Wen and me standing in the middle of the courtyard, scared stiff.

"A woman is having a difficult childbirth," she said. "This is the third day and if it goes on much longer, we'll do a Caesarean." This was a new word. Because of where I had heard it, I didn't dare ask my mother what it meant. The next day, I asked a nurse. "It's nothing you should worry about," she said, "but it's when we cut the woman's belly open to get the baby out."

I had no idea how babies were born, so I took this to be standard procedure. I ran to report to Wen who, although older than me, knew just as little about reproduction. That day we cut our dolls' stomachs open, but it took a long time to sew them back up, so we decided against performing any more Caesareans. Our dolls stayed pregnant all the time.

Sometimes a weary nurse would slosh buckets of blood into the sink in the middle of the courtyard. The first time we saw this, Wen and I looked at each other in horror and shook our heads. "I'm never going to have babies," I said solemnly.

"Me neither," she agreed. "Much too dangerous."

Another of our neighbours was a landlord who owned land in

the country and real estate in the city. Ding was strict with his wife and children, and very frugal. My mother, who spent money easily, had a theory that only people who knew how to spend knew how to earn. After Liberation, when private property was confiscated from landlords such as Ding, my mother said: "You see! We spent every penny and now we have nothing. They scrimped and saved and now they have nothing. So what was the point?"

When Wen and I reached school age we were sent to Mingming, a private primary school where the teaching was good and discipline was strict. Every morning, Amah Sun climbed into a rickshaw with us to take us to school. It was a hired rickshaw; the family's own vehicle was reserved for my mother, who needed transportation to her mahjong games. The driver was an old man with a bony frame. He seemed so fragile, but below a scrawny torso were the strong legs with which he earned his living.

I felt guilty, watching him strain as he pulled the three of us to school. In summer, it was unbearably hot work. Even in winter, sweat poured off his face as he battled against a howling northwest wind just to keep the rickshaw upright. We, meanwhile, sat snugly in the long padded coat he wrapped around us. On rainy days, a protective cloth canopy kept us dry, while he got drenched. His load must have seemed even heavier as he splashed through flooded streets. To try to make myself lighter, I sat up straight instead of lying back. Or I pressed my hands down on the seat to raise myself up a bit. When we stepped down, I tried to catch his eye and give him a smile, but he was usually hunched forward limply, giving arms and shoulders a rest.

The start of our school days introduced an unchanging routine to our lives. We got up, reluctantly in winter, in our unheated bedroom. Amah Sun served us breakfast, usually leftovers from the night before or rice porridge. Whatever we ate in the morning, it was never very nourishing; my mother believed in a light breakfast. I was usually tired and hungry long before the morning class was over. At the end of the school day, Amah Sun came back to collect us in the rickshaw. In the evening, Wen and I sat facing each other across small desks, doing our homework. No adult was ever around to help. There was such a big age gap between us and our two older sisters that they inhabited a separate world. Hua is ten years older than me; Mei, almost twenty.

Because of my reluctance to get out of bed in the morning, Wen and I were often late for class. Once we were late three days in a row. On the third day, as I was tiptoeing into the class, the teacher halted mid-sentence. "You keep coming late, Zhimei. You're disturbing the others. Come here!" My knees knocked together as I stood in front of her.

"Turn and face the class. Bow to your fellow students and ask their forgiveness." I was frightened and did as I was told. Teachers, it seemed, were not as gentle as I had thought; I now saw them as figures of authority who ought not to be offended.

The next time I saw my mother, a few days later, I told her about the incident. She was incensed. "How could she do this to my girl? To a five-year-old!" The next day, she came with us in the rickshaw to school, and marched straight to the principal's office. Wen and I, outside the door, could hear her yelling about the appalling humiliation to which our family had been subjected. She stormed out of the office angrier than when she'd stormed in, and refused to let us set foot in Mingming again.

Leaving the school marked a turning point in my life. Apart from university courses years later, the few months I spent at Mingming would be the sum total of my Chinese schooling. My education by English-speaking foreigners was about to begin.

My father had brought the family back from Japan for the sake of the children's education. But after his return he was dismayed at the quality of teaching in most schools, so he sent us all to schools run by foreign missionaries. Fees at these schools were much steeper than at public schools.

Wen and I were sent to the Catholic Sacred Heart Academy, run by the nuns of the Franciscan Missionaries of Mary. It was an imposing, three-storey building near Wangfujing, Beijing's main shopping street. It was a "ten-year" girls' school with a reputation for high-quality education and strict discipline.

In the typical missionary school in China, most teachers were Chinese and Chinese was the language of instruction. Sacred Heart was the only school in Beijing in which all the teachers were foreigners and all classes were taught in English. We were given English names: I may have been Stop Beautiful at home, but at school I was Madge. Chinese was strictly forbidden in class. If a nun overheard us speaking it in the corridor, she would remind us that English was the language of Sacred Heart.

Some of the Catholic doctrine was appealing, but I never had any desire to join the faith myself; it seemed too rigid and disciplined. But I did like the concepts of charity and of honesty. We were told to do three charitable acts a month, simple things like helping an old person cross the street or giving a few coins to a beggar. The nuns also spoke against jealousy. Because these were things taught to me by nuns, I assumed they were unique to Catholicism. Out of respect for these fine values, I also believed in their god. I believed that if we were good a guardian angel would watch over us. And I believed in the power of prayer. I prayed a lot every day: for a stomach ache to go away, for more of the cook's cornbread, for my father to be home to tell us a story over dinner.

I was really worried that Wen was going to become a nun. She often felt unfairly treated by our mother and dreamed of escaping into convent life. But in the ten years I attended Sacred Heart, only one of its Chinese students ever became a nun, and I was glad it wasn't Wen.

My parents were indifferent to the religious side of Sacred Heart. They simply wanted us to get a good education. My mother went to Wen's First Communion and was pleased with what she saw. The nuns struck her as being serious educators. It didn't matter what they were teaching us; the important thing was that they were teaching us how to learn.

Our uniform set us apart from other schoolchildren in Beijing. In winter we wore a blue dress, with white collar and cuffs. In summer, it was a white dress and a straw hat with a sky blue ribbon around its brim. One of the first things we learned at the school was how to care for our detachable collars and cuffs. After washing them, we stuck them wet on to a windowpane. By the time the sun baked them dry, they were as stiff as if they had been starched and pressed.

About a third of Sacred Heart students were foreigners. Many were the offspring of White Russians who had fled to China after the 1917 Bolshevik Revolution. Others were the children of French, Belgian, German or British missionaries. The children of U.S. army officers came later, after the Japanese surrender in 1945.

In winter, most of the foreign students wore only wool kneesocks under their dresses. They looked neat and smart, and cold. We Chinese students wore thick wool pants under our dresses and looked lumpy and clumsy. But as long as we wore our uniforms, no matter what we had on underneath, the nuns didn't object.

Discipline was strict at Sacred Heart, even in kindergarten. A nun would thunder: "Hands behind your backs, girls!" as we were marshalled into straight lines to go into the classroom. Classes started and ended with a prayer. At six years old I could recite the Lord's Prayer with perfect enunciation and absolutely no idea what it meant. The prayer at the end of the morning session seemed unbearably long as the smell of soup wafted down the hall from the dining room. At noon, Amah Sun appeared with a thermos of hot food and we ate lunch with the students who boarded at the school. One winter's day, our thermos exploded in the middle of the dining room, causing no injuries but quite a stir.

The school had a beautiful small chapel with stained-glass windows and an altar that seemed so mysterious when a service was in progress. As the priest swung the censer vigorously, he would start to disappear behind clouds of incense. I was awestruck by these strange sights and smells and felt as if I had been transported into a story from the Arabian Nights.

The nuns' lives also intrigued me. In class, I would stare at the teacher and daydream about what her life had been like before she entered the convent. If a strand of hair accidentally dangled from beneath her habit, I studied it with fascination, as if it were a rare glimpse into her curious, hidden life.

At Sacred Heart, we learned about privacy. Personal letters, for instance, were private. In most Chinese families, husbands opened their wives' mail and parents opened their children's. This was considered perfectly acceptable, a legacy of the patriarchal hierarchy of Confucianism.

We also learned about knocking at a door. You had to knock before entering if you were late for a class. When the nun opened the door, you were to ask: "May I come in?" In a Chinese school, you simply opened the door and crept in. At home we walked in and out of each other's rooms without knocking. Doors were usually left open, anyway, and closed only at night or if we were sick.

When we were young we locked our bedroom door during the day only when we were up to no good: tearing a toy apart or putting on mother's face powder. Amah Sun was always suspicious of a closed door and would yell to us from the other side: "Stop whatever you're doing in there!" If our mother's bedroom door was shut during the day, it meant she had been out late the night before playing mahjong and we knew we had to keep quiet.

My first taste of Western literature was at Sacred Heart. We had a small library with simplified versions of classic novels, including my favourites, *Jane Eyre* and *Wuthering Heights*. Jane Eyre was my heroine: I was impressed by her strong will and experience of romantic love. I read the novel three times, and later read it again when a Chinese translation was published.

At the end of the month, Mother Notker stood near the only exit as we filed out and gave us each a reminder to bring in the next month's tuition. Everyone was afraid of the way she peered over her spectacles as she spoke. To me she often said: "Yours was late last month, Madge. Try to be on time."

But when Beijing was under siege in late 1948 and early 1949, "Mother Bill Collector" lost all her severity. Those were the final days of nationalist rule; communist troops had encircled the capital. My father had been out of work for four years. My mother had tried to make ends meet by taking in sewing, but we never had quite enough money.

"Mother Notker, I won't be able to come to school on Monday. My mother says she can't afford the fees this month."

She patted me on the shoulder. "Madge, you've been at Sacred Heart since kindergarten. We can't have you not finishing your schooling. It's a special situation now and you should come to school as usual." Her words made me feel, for the first time, that I really belonged at the school.

After the Japanese surrender of 1945, the families of U.S. army officers began arriving in Beijing in their hundreds. The officers had been sent to monitor a short-lived armistice agreement between the nationalists and communists. Suddenly, Sacred Heart was full of boisterous, chatty American girls. I envied them. They all seemed so rich. They ate chocolate bars and chewed gum, something we had never seen before. They dressed well and disliked wearing a uniform, so the nuns relaxed the dress code and now even allowed slacks.

Once a staid parochial school, Sacred Heart would never be the same. Older Chinese girls started dating American soldiers. We called them "jeep girls" because GIs picked them up after school in jeeps. They often got into trouble with the nuns for being late to school because they had stayed out late the night before. But I envied them, too; they seemed so grown up and to be having so much fun.

I often went window-shopping after school with a Chinese classmate the nuns called Elizabeth. One afternoon, as we were wandering through an indoor market, the lights went out. Power cuts had been frequent during the Japanese occupation and merchants had grown accustomed to setting a candle on the edge of their stalls. In the darkness I saw Elizabeth grab handfuls of peanuts from a stall and stuff them in her pockets. The nuns had drilled "thou shalt not steal" into us along with the other commandments. But Elizabeth walked away nonchalantly and refused to admit what she had done. Girls at school began complaining that they were losing things. One day, I happened to see Elizabeth rifling through our coats.

"I saw what you did in the cloakroom," I said to her later during a break between classes.

She turned red. "You're a liar! It's not Christian, you know, you shouldn't tell lies. But then, you non-believers are all big liars. Anyway, how can you prove what you've said?"

I hated myself for not knowing how to make the others believe me, and I started to cry. A nun came into the classroom and demanded to know what was happening. She called me to the front. "Madge, you know you shouldn't make this kind of accusation without being able to prove it. I think you owe Elizabeth an apology."

Suddenly, I was on trial and Elizabeth was coming off as the injured party. In anger and frustration, I started to pull at my uniform as my sniffles turned to wild sobs. A piece of my dress ripped and I tore at it. Soon I was tearing my dress apart in front of a hushed classroom. Eventually, I stood in woollen leggings and undershirt, a shredded dress at my feet.

The nun was startled and sent me home. When my sister Hua heard the story, she gave me a sisterly scolding that I would never forget. "What a spineless creature! Why did you accuse her like that if you weren't prepared to back up what you said, to stick up for yourself, to fight!" I knew she had a point. I had a rebellious spirit, but it was not matched by an equal measure of self-assertive combativeness. It was an important lesson.

The incident was never mentioned again, but I felt a cloud hanging over me at school. I couldn't understand why the nuns let

Elizabeth get away with habitual petty theft when they were constantly niggling at me to sit up straight in class, walk softly in the chapel, eat my food without slurping.

One day, after the Japanese surrender, my former friend Elizabeth pointed at me and said in front of other classmates: "What have *you* got to be proud of now? Your father is a *hanjian*."

That meant "traitor to China," but why had she said it? I went home and asked my mother.

"Don't listen to her, Zhimei. There are people who for some reason take pleasure in other people's misfortune." She did not elaborate. It was my first introduction to the "bad" family background that was to dog me in China for the next four decades.

Chapter Three

QUICK! LOCK UP THE GIRLS!

CRASH!!

After the room-shaking thud came a tinkling of broken glass. I raced into the living room. Our old grandfather clock lay on its side, face shattered, shiny wooden frame cracked and splintered. My mother stood beside it, shaking with fury. The clock had been a fixture in our home, but it seemed she had deliberately toppled it. Had she gone mad?

"I've had enough! I'd rather break it to pieces than sell it for so little," she howled. "Every day the drumbeater takes something away. What will we have left?"

Junk collectors were called drumbeaters because as they wandered through Beijing's alleys they beat a tiny drum about two inches in diameter. Two enormous bamboo baskets swung from their shoulder poles. They collected almost anything people wanted to unload: antiques were most desirable, then clothes, then odds and ends of any kind. If you had furniture for them, they came back later pulling a flatbed cart. In the years just before Liberation, it was not unusual for us to buy our food with money received the same day from the drumbeater.

Our carved mahogany furniture, carpets, sofas, fine china and works of art had all been taken away, item by item. For me, it was a nuisance when a useful piece of furniture vanished from its familiar spot; for my mother, it was also adding up to an unbearable personal loss.

The day before she toppled the clock, the piano had been sold. Mei's two-year-old son was heartbroken. He threw himself at one of the drumbeaters who was struggling the piano out the door. Clutching the man's leg, he sobbed: "Please don't take away our singing horse (as he called it). Please!" Wen, who used to play the piano every evening after supper, looked on sadly. My father sat quietly in a corner, puffing nervously on his pipe. It was painful to watch him these days. He was talking less and less.

During the piano removal, my mother had seemed matter-of-fact about the situation. "This is no house for a piano, much too damp. If we keep it any longer it will be ruined and we won't be able to get a good price for it." But the next day, as she stood alone in an almost empty living room, the loss sank in. Something snapped in her and she gave the clock a shove.

She started asking me to call in the junk collector. The task had become too mortifying to do herself. My sisters felt the same way, but I was too young to understand this kind of humiliation. I didn't mind running out to find the drumbeater when we heard him entering the neighbourhood.

Hua sold her vast record collection, disk after treasured disk. One day she would hand over an album of Strauss waltzes. The next day she would have to part with Handel's *Messiah*. As for the records my father had brought back from Japan, there was no market for them. The Japanese occupation had only just ended and no one wanted to be reminded of it. So we softened the records in hot water and shaped them into containers of various kinds. We kept peanuts in one such bowl.

Hua tried to hang on to her pictures of Hollywood movie stars, but soon even they were gone. Her collection had grown to 300 pictures which she kept neatly in silk-covered boxes. She never tired of taking out a stack of pictures and explaining which movies the stills were from. Her pride and joy were the ones from *Gone with the Wind.* My own ideal images of male and female beauty were shaped by the faces in Hua's collection.

I started to develop a loathing for the drumbeaters the day one came back to ask if we had more of the movie-star pictures. They sold really well, he said. I drove him out. Those pictures had been precious to Hua and it had pained her to hand them over.

Times had started to get tough after the Japanese surrender, an otherwise happy event that spelled the end of my father's career. After working for several years at the Construction Ministry, in 1941 he had been transferred to the North China Wheat Association, which was responsible for wheat processing in the region. After he lost that job in 1945, because he had been employed by the Japanese he never again had steady work. He gradually sank into obscurity, even within the family. When he wasn't around, we never talked about him. There didn't seem to be anything to say.

Politics were rarely discussed in my family, and I knew little about what was going on outside our house. But suddenly there were big changes even inside the home. No longer able to afford the rent on the big house, we dismissed the servants and moved into a place that was one-seventh the size.

"You really are a good-for-nothing!" my mother muttered to my father. "Look at our neighbours! They all own mansions." Although we had been well off, we were never wealthy enough to own a house.

The new place was located in an alley near Wangfujing, close to Sacred Heart. All the rooms faced north, so we no longer had sunny spots to sit in. Every day we chopped firewood, shovelled coal into the house and dumped out the cinders from the day before. The new house had no bathtub or running water. We shared a tap in the courtyard with three other families. In winter, our hands became chapped and blistered from rinsing clothes and dishes in the icy water. I felt embarrassed one day when a boy held my hand and I realized how rough mine was compared with his.

The house also had no indoor toilet. Two big vats buried in the ground functioned as latrines. People of the same sex would squat side by side and carry on long conversations. In summer, the odour became unbearable in between the nightsoil collector's weekly visits. We threw lime around the edges of the buried vats to stop the maggots ascending. My mother refused to use these facilities, preferring to keep a chamber pot in her bedroom.

Our nightsoil collector was a good-natured man with a misshapen face. Adults called him by his nickname, "manure monkey," behind his back, but children taunted him with it to his face. Normally he ignored them, but if they kept up an incessant chorus, he knew how to silence them: "If you call me that one more time, I'll wipe my shit ladle on you!"

I felt sorry for him as I watched him lumbering under the heavy wooden barrel he carried over his shoulder and emptied into a bigger vessel on a wooden handcart. Sometimes I saw the contents of the barrel overflowing down his back. Women would cover their noses and quicken their step when he approached. Nightsoil collectors, who were mostly poor, illiterate men from the countryside, were often not able to find a wife because of the lowly status of their thankless job. The "manure despots" who controlled the nightsoil men made a fortune by exploiting them.

Even after our move to this more modest house, without my father's income our meagre savings began to disappear.

My mother managed to wean herself almost totally off mahjong as the family fortunes plummeted. She cut back from playing every day to once a month, and now for much lower stakes.

After my father lost his job, he seemed to accept the defeat in a passive way that irritated us all. I had very ambivalent feelings toward him. At times I blamed him for what I saw as his weakness; at other times I felt more charitable and bitterly resented all the humiliation he was made to suffer. He did make one last stab at improving our lot but it was an abject failure. He bought a pear orchard just outside Beijing and was pleased with himself after striking the deal. What a fantastic bargain! But that summer, he discovered why: the orchard bore no fruit. He couldn't sell it for even a fraction of what he had paid. When prospective buyers asked about the yield, he couldn't lie.

Meanwhile, inflation was also devouring our savings. It spiralled out of control in the last stages of the civil war. In 1935, the Kuomintang government had issued a banknote called a *fabi*. By August 1948, the fabi had become so worthless that when the government issued a new banknote called a *jinyuanjuan*, the exchange rate was one jinyuanjuan to three million fabi. But the new currency devalued even faster. An item that had cost one new jinyuanjuan cost 1.2 million just ten months later. A sack of flour now cost a sack of money.

People with money bought gold and silver. Pilots in the Kuomintang air force went into the gold business; it was rumoured that planes had crashed because they were overloaded with gold. Pilots walked around with sheaves of banknotes bulging ostentatiously out of hip pockets. When Hua returned from Tianjin to Beijing after her marriage to a middle-ranking Kuomintang officer, she hid twenty ounces of gold, part of her husband's savings, inside her bra.

Buying and selling silver *yuan* was another popular way to profiteer. A silver-yuan black market sprang up just off Wangfujing. Traders struck their bargains inside the long baggy sleeves of their traditional gowns. One man would squeeze another man's hand a certain number of times to indicate the buying or selling price he was offering. The second man would make his counteroffer in the same way.

The negotiations and the transaction were well concealed inside the sleeves. But checking whether the silver was "good coin" had to be done on the outside. The prospective buyer would hold the coin by the edges, between thumb and forefinger. He would blow forcefully along one edge and then place it quickly to the ear. Experienced traders could detect non-silver content by the sound. The Wangfujing silver market was still active in the first year after

Liberation. The communists, with a lot of other things on their minds, tolerated it for a while.

After my father lost his job, there was one last lavish event in the family: Hua's marriage to the Kuomintang officer. A family friend had introduced her to Yu, whose regiment was stationed in Tianjin. They were married in the fall of 1948, in a Western-style wedding. Yu paid for it all, a decadent affair held in the big dance hall of a fancy hotel. Guests danced to a Big Band and the groom got drunk. Despite her wedding finery, which included a long white gown, Hua looked sombre. She wasn't in love. She thought that by marrying this wealthy Kuomintang officer, she was helping out our whole family.

In late 1948, just weeks after Hua's wedding, the communist Eighth Route Army had Kuomintang-controlled Beijing under siege. Electrical and water supplies were cut. The periodic blackouts so frequent during the occupation became perpetual. We heard gunfire in the distance as the two sides battled it out. Meanwhile, negotiations for the city's peaceful liberation were also under way.

Although we no longer had running water in our courtyard, we were lucky to have a well nearby. It was located at the end of our lane, aptly called Big Sweet Water Well Alley. First thing in the morning we would join the line and draw enough water to see us through the day. It was a treacherous task because the area around the well was slippery with ice.

Grain became scarce. All that could be had in the stores was a coarse mixture of sorghum and maize ground together with beans and sweet potatoes. It was gritty and close to black in colour; bread made from it was as hard as stone when cold. There was no more talk in those days about what was and wasn't good for a young lady's digestion.

My mother accompanied Hua to Tianjin, where the fighting was particularly intense. My sister, along with other Kuomintang army dependants, was supposed to retreat to Guangdong province. But when she got to Tianjin she decided not to go and the last ship carrying evacuees left without her. Then the railway to Beijing was cut, and Hua and my mother were stuck in Tianjin. They stayed with a friend in the British concession. The battle noises were distant until street fighting began near where they were staying, but it lasted only a day. The communists took Tianjin on January 14, 1949, with few casualties.

Several weeks after the liberation of Tianjin, my mother and Hua took the first available train back to Beijing but it could only go as far as Fengtai. They took a pedicab the rest of the way, riding against a cold February wind. What would have been a fifteen-minute train ride took more than two hours. By the time they made it home, Beijing, too, had been liberated.

Back in Beijing in the last few weeks before Liberation, there was nothing to do. Sacred Heart was closed for the long winter holidays that extended from Christmas until after Chinese New Year in February. With no lights, the evenings seemed endless. My father tried his best to keep us amused playing cards by a dim oil lamp. Gunfire and explosions off in the distance provided dramatic sound effects for our nightly card games. One night, a bomb went off at the home of the mayor of Beijing. He and his French wife survived, but a daughter was killed.

One evening we heard an insistent pounding at the gate. By that time four families were living in our courtyard house, but no one dared open up. "Hurry up! Open the door!" The voices on the other side sounded scared. We guessed they were disbanded Kuomintang, terrified young soldiers on the run. But we feared that although they were ostensibly looking for food and shelter, they were really after women and money.

"Quick!" said my eldest sister, Mei. "Lock up the girls in the room behind the mirror."

The mirror on the door to one small room made it look from the outside like a wardrobe. My father did not let the soldiers into the house until my sisters and I were safely locked away.

Three Kuomintang soldiers burst into the house. "We just want a place to sleep," one of them said. "And we need food, too. We're starving."

My father gave them what little we had. After the warm meal, they collapsed on the floor and slept with their clothes on. My father covered them with our quilts. Packed into our crowded hiding place, my sisters and I whispered nervously late into the night. My father and Mei's husband stayed up the whole night guarding us against attack. But the soldiers were not as horrible as expected and the night passed uneventfully. Early the next morning they departed, having done no more harm than leaving lice behind on the quilts.

The sound of distant gunfire continued for many days. One day the battle noises stopped; not owning a radio, we didn't know what had happened. It was all very confusing: some neighbours brought back snippets of real news and others brought back wildly unreliable rumours. Who could tell one from the other? A lot was rumoured about the Eighth Route Army. The communists, it was said, want to share everything you have — your house, your land, your wife. The adults were all saying these things, so we children repeated them too.

One day, word got back to our courtyard that tanks had appeared in the streets and that the soldiers were wearing big fur coats and hats, the likes of which were not worn in Beijing. Their clothing gave them away: they were the communist advance troops sent down from the already liberated northeast to prepare for the taking of Beijing. History-making events quite aside, we begged to be allowed to go out to see those fur coats. My father relented; we had been cooped up for so long.

"But don't go near them!" he warned. "We don't know their behaviour, and anything could happen to you."

Like birds out of a cage, Wen and I flew out of the house. Apart from the odd bicycle or rickshaw, the streets were deserted. Three tanks were parked on one street, the tank drivers sitting up on top.

Small groups of people stood at a cautious distance, staring at the soldiers with curiosity and unease.

They looked nice enough to me. Wen and I edged closer. I smiled at one of the soldiers and got a friendly nod in return. "You see!" I whispered to Wen. "They're not monsters!" That was my first impression of the communist troops.

Beijing was liberated that day – January 31, 1949. It was a peaceful transfer of power, without casualties or chaos. Whatever was left by the last emperor and not looted by the Kuomintang remained undamaged. The communist troops carried on towards the south to liberate other areas of China.

At Liberation, after twenty-one years of being called Beiping, the city reverted to its original name, Beijing, which means "northern capital." The Nationalists had named it Beiping ("northern peace") when they set up their own capital at Nanjing ("southern capital").

When my mother and Hua boarded the first train out of Tianjin, they left in a rush, without knowing what had become of Hua's husband, Yu. Three months after the taking of Tianjin, he turned up in Beijing. He had completed a "re-education course" and been given a travel permit to the capital, but no guarantee of work there. High-ranking Kuomintang officers were imprisoned after Liberation, some for three decades. They were gradually released over the years; the last were set free in a 1980 amnesty. But there were too many foot soldiers to imprison, so they and middle-ranking officers were "re-educated" and let go.

Yu couldn't find work in Beijing and after several months he and Hua departed for his native Guangdong province. But six months later Hua returned to Beijing, alone and pregnant. Her son was born on October 1, 1950, the first anniversary of the founding of the People's Republic. She never saw Yu again. It had been a hasty marriage and she found they had nothing in common.

Life gradually returned to normal. Sacred Heart re-opened, although not exactly as its old self. In earlier times of turmoil, politics were as little discussed within the school compound as they were in our courtyard home. Many parents, anxious to shield their children from the occupation and civil war, had liked the sequestered nature of Sacred Heart.

But after Liberation, not even Sacred Heart could maintain its insularity. Students from Qinghua, the most prestigious university in Beijing, came to the school and organized the two senior classes into study groups. The university students' objectives were to set our thinking straight and to change our curriculum. They distributed pamphlets of works by Mao, Marx and Engels, Lenin and Stalin. We met in discussion groups to study the *Communist Manifesto* and various Maoist tracts.

I found the vocabulary in those Chinese-language pamphlets more difficult than in the Catholic catechism because at that point I could read English more easily than Chinese. There were many mysterious new words: proletariat, bourgeoisie, class struggle, exploitation, people's democratic dictatorship and all the "isms." I tried to make up for my silence in the group discussions by being enthusiastic about other tasks. I cut out characters from red paper to hang as slogans on the classroom walls with as much fervour as anyone.

We were to understand two things. First, the education we had received from missionaries was tantamount to cultural invasion by foreign powers. Second: there was no God.

We were encouraged to criticize our educational background and to acknowledge that our minds had been poisoned by it. We were taken to mass gatherings on campuses to hear students make flamboyant speeches about communism. We were drilled in the lyrics of revolutionary songs.

At one mass meeting on the campus of Beijing University, hundreds of students sat around a huge bonfire. Impassioned orators mesmerized us with speeches about the bright communist future. And then we belted out the new songs we had learned: "The sky in the liberated area is bright and clear/The people in the liberated area are so happy / A democratic government loves the people / We can never thank the People's Liberation Army enough."

I had never had such powerful experiences. Everything was so intense: the passion of the speeches, the camaraderie. These students had an ideal. Although I did not totally understand what it was they were striving for, I was inspired by their ardour.

The basement at Sacred Heart, which had once been our playroom, was now a "base for revolutionary activities." We wrote posters critical of the school: "Why isn't Chinese history taught here?" "Why isn't Chinese spoken here?" We wrote them in English so the nuns could read them.

We became convinced we really were victims of imperialist cultural aggression, our minds invaded by foreign ideas. One student refused to wear her Sacred Heart uniform any more and now came to school in a long, traditional scholar's gown. The school authorities took all this in silence and did not interfere.

One day shortly after the start of our 1950 summer holidays, Wen and I both received our graduation diplomas in the mail. This was strange, because Wen was in the graduating year, but I was not. I had just turned 15 and still had a year to go. But the nuns had decided to let the two senior classes graduate at once. This was the least provocative way they could think of to expel both classes. We had become a nuisance with our political posters and study sessions, and they had had enough.

The students in my year, under the guidance of the Qinghua University activists, mounted a fresh protest. In this round of posters we argued that foreign nuns had no right to expel Chinese students from a school in China. But the nuns stood their ground.

Sacred Heart continued to accept Chinese students for two years after Liberation. Then enrolment was restricted to the children of foreign diplomats. The nuns rarely ventured out of the compound any more. The statue of the Virgin Mary recessed into the school's facade and the crucifix on top of the building remained in place for almost two decades after Liberation. But during the Cultural Revolution they were smashed and the nuns chased out of China as spies. The Municipal Textile Bureau occupied the building for a while, but Beijing's Sacred Heart is now no longer standing.

"What's the use of girls going to college anyway? Can't you see we're living from hand to mouth as it is?" My mother and Wen were having a familiar battle. For a year, over our mother's objections, Wen had been going to college. But in the summer of 1951, she fought a last round on the issue and lost. She would have to find a job.

That was also the end of my dream to continue studying. I spent almost a year after graduation lounging around gathering dust. As summer drifted into autumn, I sat for hours each day in my old spot in the courtyard. I was bored, and my imagination could no longer conjure up something amusing to project on to the brick wall in front of me. The turtles in their straw hats who had kept me entertained as a child were gone. Instead, I projected my own listlessness on to the world. The rustling of fallen leaves sounded like a dirge; the chirping of birds, spiritless and unmelodious.

To relieve the boredom, Wen and I would occasionally go out dancing with friends. Most dance halls went out of business after Liberation, but two were still operating near our house in 1950. The room would be dimly lit by red and blue bulbs as a band of five or six musicians played the songs of Bing Crosby, the Andrews Sisters or Frank Sinatra.

I also saw many Western films in this period, including *Bathing Beauty* with Esther Williams, *For Whom the Bell Tolls* starring Ingrid Bergman, and Charlie Chaplin's *Gold Rush*. But a few years after Liberation, Hollywood films were replaced by Soviet ones. The suave, seductive Americans we were used to watching were suddenly replaced by plump, hard-working commune members. Svelte bathing beauties were out; tractor drivers with ruddy cheeks and flower-patterned kerchiefs were in.

"I can't stand those round, red-tomato faces," a male friend complained after seeing too many Soviet films.

One day a family friend mentioned that the National Import Corporation had just moved to Beijing from Tianjin and was recruiting. My mother took me there the next day. Half a dozen applicants were already waiting when we arrived. They looked much older and more self-possessed than me. I chose a chair in a dark corner, where I fidgeted nervously until my turn came.

A middle-aged man in a Mao jacket called me into his office. "First of all, can you write something in English about your background?" he asked.

"I've written something already," I said. My sisters had told me to expect that. The previous evening I had written a page and a half in simple, childish English. Although he couldn't read English, he was impressed. He looked at me sceptically. "Did you really write this yourself? How long have you studied English?"

"Ten years. I started in kindergarten."

"What school did you go to?"

I hesitated. There was a time when I had been proud to say I studied at Sacred Heart, proud of the solid education the name implied. After Liberation, I was ashamed to mention the fact. Educated by missionaries? That made me practically a foreign product, head stuffed with bourgeois ideas!

But I couldn't lie. When I told him, he just nodded. I was relieved. He seemed most interested in seeking assurance that I had written the text I had given him. A Sacred Heart education was confirmation enough.

"Now let's see if you can type," he said.

I had taken a three-month typing course and so wasn't worried about this part of the interview. He gave me a clean sheet of paper and a text to copy on a 1930s Underwood. Then he positioned himself close behind me, holding a stopwatch.

When he clicked it on, my fingers froze. When they did begin to move, they hit the wrong keys. I had needed glasses for some time, but we couldn't afford them. My myopia must have been apparent as I bent close to the text and the keyboard. I seemed to spend more time furiously backspacing to correct mistakes than typing forward. At the end of the five-minute test, I was ashamed of the messy sheet I had produced.

"How did it go?" my mother asked on our way home. She could have read the answer on my face.

"Not a chance," I said, fighting tears. "I think the examiner took me for a child. And I botched the typing test."

Early the next morning, as I began the housework that obviously was going to be my lot in life, a motorbike screeched to a halt in front of our gate. In strode a young man in a messenger's outfit with a big envelope in his hand.

"Anyone here by the name of Zhang Zhimei?" he asked. Sure enough, there on the envelope was my name and, in the right-hand corner, the characters for "urgent." I ran inside and tore it open. For such a big envelope, it contained a short message. "You are hired. Report for work tomorrow at 8:00 a.m." I gave a whoop. My working life was about to begin! I felt very grown up.

The Import Corporation was on the other side of the city. I had no idea how long the tram ride would take in the early morning and didn't want to be late. When I woke at 5:00 a.m., hours before my alarm went off, the moon was still hanging in a cold February sky. My mother, who had never in her life prepared breakfast for us, called out from her bed: "Fix yourself something hot, Zhimei. And dress warmly. You've got a long ride ahead of you."

My father crawled out of bed and stoked the fire. We said nothing while I got myself ready. I wondered if he could hear my nerves jangling in the silence.

"I'm going, Pa." He stood up without a word and followed me to the gate.

"It's cold. You'd better go inside, Pa."

"No, no. I'll watch you go."

I walked a dozen paces and turned around with the idea of giving a cheery wave. But I stopped myself. My father looked so forlorn.

All the worries of recent years were written in wrinkles on his face. A threadbare coat hung loosely on his thin frame. My eyes fell on his old cotton shoes. "Can this be the same dad who could once liven up the dinner table with his stories?"

I knew that as he watched me go off to work, he was feeling like a failure. He had lost the last job he would have and as a result I was starting my first one at an early age. He knew how much I had wanted to go to college. I wanted to say something, but the words wouldn't come. I wanted to tell him not to feel guilty, that I understood. I wanted to tell him that a girl could be just as useful to a family as a boy, and that I was going to prove it to him.

"I'm not a bit afraid, Pa. It's o.k." I actually was very afraid, and sorry that neither of us could express our real feelings. I turned abruptly and walked away. Before rounding the corner, I looked back. There was my father in the distance, still standing motionless in the shadow of a dim streetlight.

After Liberation, my father had been afraid to get a job. And his instincts may have been right; if he had had a job he could well have been caught up in the political campaigns of the 1950s, and then banished to a remote place or persecuted to death, as were many of his former colleagues. Because he had only been a civilian official under the Japanese, and not involved in military or political affairs, he was left more or less alone after Liberation. It also would have been a different story if he had made money illegally or by exploiting his fellow Chinese or by speculating on the stock market. My mother once cursed the fact that we were not wealthy enough to own a mansion; after Liberation, she thanked her lucky stars.

The tram ride seemed long. Except for street cleaners and workers just off the night shift, the streets were empty. It took twenty minutes to walk from the tram stop to the Import Corporation, which was located in what must have been an opulent mansion before Liberation. Buildings were grouped around a network of courtyards that stretched back from the front gate. It was the sort of place my family had once lived in.

In the second courtyard I saw a sign for the Secretarial Department, where I was supposed to report. When I pulled open the door, acrid smoke stung my eyes. Through the cloud I could make out the figure of a young boy, squatting to light a stove.

"Leave the door open," he yelled. Then he sauntered over to examine me. "Who are you?"

"I'm a newcomer."

"That figures! Nobody comes to work this early. You'll have to wait outside until I finish cleaning the place." At that, the first English typist ever hired by the China National Import Corporation slunk back out into the courtyard and waited in the bitter cold.

At the end of my first month of work, I learned what my salary would be: 320 jin (160 kilos) of millet a month. The new regime was trying to stabilize prices and in the first few years after Liberation salaries were linked to the value of millet. We did not actually receive 320 jin of the grain, but its fluctuating cash value. My pay varied a little every month, but usually I received about thirty-two yuan. I made more than the other typists because I was working in English and they in Chinese.

My first pay cheque seemed an incredible fortune. When I got home I ran to find my mother who, as usual, was bent over her sewing machine. "Here's my first pay, Ma!"

She stopped pedalling for a moment and looked up at me. "We don't need the money. Go get yourself a pair of glasses."

I didn't want to hurt her pride by forcing the money on her, but I knew we did need my pay. She worked day in, day out at her sewing machine, making children's clothes to sell to stores. But we could still hardly make ends meet.

First I ran to the store and bought some treats for dinner: a smoked chicken and a cream cake. Then I bought my first pair of glasses, the ordinary kind that had clear plastic frames with a hint of pink. I thought a more stylish pair would look unsuitable perched on the nose of a dedicated worker in a state-run corporation.

We all felt very proud to be working for the government, to have been invited into the revolutionary ranks, and we dressed the part. "Lenin jackets" were popular, especially among women. Perhaps they were so named because of their collars, which were more Western-looking than those on Mao jackets. Of grey or blue cotton, the double-breasted Lenin jacket had a belt and so a more shapely look than the Mao jacket. With my pigtails coiled up under a grey cap, I felt the effect was quite chic.

One afternoon a week, the canteen at work was transformed into a lecture hall. The tables were removed, and the corporation's 120 workers sat in rows along back-less benches. These political-study sessions consumed a full afternoon, with an interminable lecture followed by rambling group discussion.

The first lecture I attended promised to cover a fair bit of ground: "Survey of the Development of Society from the Primitive to the Communist." At first, the speaker's eloquence impressed me and for two hours I paid close attention. Others around me were even more attentive, and many took notes. But as the speaker plunged into his third hour, his own enthusiasm for historical materialism still undiminished, he lost me. I took from my bag the book I had brought for the tram ride and began reading. A few people looked around in surprise. But the way I saw it, it was either read my book quietly or be put to sleep and fall face forwards off the bench.

The next morning as I entered the compound, a crowd was examining the bulletin board inside the front gate. "What's up?" I asked a man at the back of the group.

He recognized me and grinned. "Have a look for yourself!"

I eased myself through the crowd. A caricature was up on the board: a slim girl with long pigtails and a pair of tight pants sat on a backless bench, her nose in a book. Other figures drawn around her were leaning forward, listening attentively.

I couldn't believe my eyes. "Why am I up there?" I asked the man beside me. "It's a form of criticism," he said gently. It was clear that I would have to think of other ways of keeping awake at political study sessions.

A few months later, I had my first introduction to a political campaign. As a test of loyalty, we were to open our hearts to the party and reveal all about our past. The idea was to teach us not to keep secrets from the party. Official circulars promised "leniency toward those who confess and severity to those who hold back."

People pulled the skeletons out of their closets and put them on public display without giving much thought to possible consequences. No one had any experience yet with the "free speech" campaigns that backfired. Li spoke about his years as a Kuomintang foot soldier before Liberation; Jiang had worked for a foreign company; Peng had been a sailor on a foreign cargo ship; Chen had had two wives. Many people wept as they earnestly told their stories and asked to be pardoned by the party.

I knew all about Confession from my years at Sacred Heart, although there, you didn't have to bare your soul in public. I racked my brain. I know! I had lied about my age at my job interview. Not wanting to be rejected because of my youth, I had told them I was eighteen, when in fact I was only sixteen. What a relief! I had something to confess. My first public self-criticism was greeted with much giggling from my co-workers. But the party official in charge of recording our confessions in our dossiers curtly silenced them and praised the "correct attitude" that had prompted my admission.

One afternoon a meeting was called at short notice. Once we were assembled, the head of the personnel department walked in carrying a sheaf of dossiers. He sat at a table at the front of the room, looking stern.

"Most people have behaved correctly in the loyalty campaign. But there have been exceptions." He paused to allow the menacing impact of the statement to register. "At least one person has refused to confess." That was the cue for two security police to appear. They walked up to a man in the audience, yanked him roughly to his feet and handcuffed him.

"This is what we mean by severity to those who refuse to

confess," the cadre continued in a cold, measured voice. "Yuan once belonged to the Kuomintang youth group and he tried to conceal this fact. It would not have been a problem if he had been open about it, you understand. His crime was in trying to keep it secret from the party."

He pulled three files from his stack, moving deliberately, building the tension. "The party knows of a few others who have been holding back. Do not underestimate the party's policy on this matter. Do not underestimate its power." It was a terrifying scene, which, of course, it was intended to be.

Not long after this meeting I received word that Shen, the director of the corporation, wanted to see me. Haunted by the handcuffing scene, I was worried. What past crime had I failed to confess? My heart was pounding as I made my way to his office.

After I was ushered in, the director got right to the point. "How would you like to go abroad?"

I was stunned. It was not what I had expected. I hesitated, afraid to betray my excitement. If I showed how much I wanted to go, wherever it was, then perhaps he would change his mind. I tried to sound earnest but nonchalant.

"I'd be happy to go wherever the party thinks I would be most useful," I said.

"How would you feel about leaving your parents? After all, you're only sixteen."

"I'm really quite independent."

"I've noticed," he said, and paused. The suspense was killing me. Now my heart was racing with excitement, not fear.

"I'm going to assign you to the trade delegation leaving in two months for East Germany," Shen said at last. "I myself will be leading it. We need an English typist and you're the only one available." With that, the one-minute meeting that changed my life was over.

Chapter Four

SLOW DANCING IN EAST BERLIN

The opportunity to live in a foreign country was exciting. But by far the more thrilling prospect was the pre-departure shopping spree. Every member of a government delegation being posted abroad was given 600 yuan to buy a new wardrobe. This was an unimaginable fortune, almost two years' salary. The government wanted to spruce us up before sending us out into the world; it was a matter of national pride that we should look presentable.

Clothes stores didn't know what hit them when, in the fall of 1951, a middle-aged man shepherding six young women suddenly appeared and cleared them out of their best stock. A cadre was assigned to go shopping with us, the six typists being sent to various Eastern Europe countries. We needed clothes for all occasions and seasons. I had four *qipao* made, the close-fitting traditional gowns that I never had occasion to wear in Beijing. One was black satin, another lined for winter wear. We bought everything from underwear to the one imitation fur coat we were each allowed.

None of us had ever had clothes made to measure before. We leafed through the 1940s Western catalogues at the tailors and were spellbound. It *all* looked so gorgeous. We were not used to such choice, and agonized for hours over each decision about style, fabric and colour. Even the everyday items we already had just wouldn't do. We bought new supplies of toothpaste and soap. We wanted new *everything*. We bought two new suitcases each to hold the bounty. It felt as if we were gathering a dowry.

We also attended classes on how to behave in a foreign culture. I jotted down the essentials:

- Do not lick your knife
- Do not scratch your scalp during negotiating sessions with foreigners
- Do not bite your fingernails when talking to foreigners
- Do not spit in the street
- Cover your mouth when you sneeze or yawn
- Women enter first, be it a room or a car.

We were drilled on other rules as well. Those of us headed for Berlin were briefed on the complicated situation in which the city was divided into an eastern and western section. The most important thing to remember was that never, under any circumstances, were we to stray into the western half. Nor were we even to venture out alone on to the streets of East Berlin; we were always to travel in pairs or groups.

On the mild November evening of my departure, I choked down a farewell supper with my family. No one said much. My parents were not demonstrative by nature, but I knew they were proud of me – chosen, still a teenager, for a foreign assignment. I was glad the lightbulb on the porch needed replacing, so that no one could see me wiping my eyes as I walked away with Hua. She rode the tram with me to a hostel where I would spend the night. My group would leave from there early the next morning. At the hostel, I changed out of my old clothes and gave them to Hua to take home. From tomorrow onward, I would wear only new things.

"You're on your own now, Zhimei," Hua said in parting. "Don't do anything stupid. Try to learn how to behave like an adult." Spoken like an older sister – but how I would miss her! I wept a little after she left, then made a mighty effort to pull myself together. I was not only leaving home for the first time, but also the country, and I was scared.

The next morning we flew from Beijing to the Mongolian capital of Ulan Bator on a Soviet airplane. I had never flown before and didn't dare look out of the window. A colleague assured me I hadn't missed much, just vast stretches of snow and ice. I closed my eyes and tried hard not to think about how foolish it was to entrust your life to a metal container suspended in mid-air. I refused to eat, sure that I would be sick if I did.

The hotel we stayed at for a night in Ulan Bator was clean and comfortable. But the toilet facilities were primitive, even by Chinese standards. You had to feel your way through deep snow in the pitch dark out to a rickety outhouse. I felt just a little too close to nature as I answered its call that night, with the temperature hovering around minus thirty degrees Celsius and the howling pack of dogs I could hear in the distance drawing nearer.

The next day we continued on to Moscow. During the fraternal 1950s, Chinese delegations on their way to posts in Eastern Europe always broke up their trip in the Soviet capital for a week of sightseeing and briefings. We then took the train to East Berlin, where we were installed at Hotel Johanneshof. It was the best hotel in East Berlin, and within walking distance of the West. At the time, only checkpoints divided the city; the Wall would go up a decade later. If we got off at the wrong stop on the subway, called the U-Bahn, we could easily end up in the West. We were warned of that danger on the day of our arrival.

At first, our twenty-member delegation was responsible for handling trade relations with East Germany alone. About a year later, the group was reorganized, with half to be responsible for trade with East-Bloc countries and the other half to deal with businessmen from Western Europe. I was in the second group. If Western Europeans wanted to do business with the new China, they had to come to see us in East Berlin.

Working and living spaces combined, we occupied half the

second floor of the hotel. We were assigned a simply furnished single or double room on the basis of rank. Being the youngest member of the delegation, I had a roommate: Feng, a Chinese-language typist who was one year older than me and who became a close friend.

The dining-room on the second floor was reserved for our delegation. I was not very impressed with German food, except for the rolls smeared with butter and sausages slathered in mustard. I topped off every meal with a bowl of ice-cream. I also ate chocolate cake and ice cream regularly at breakfast. None of us had a very good grasp of what foods foreigners ate at what meals. In China, our breakfasts consisted of whatever was around, usually leftovers from the day before. I soon outgrew many of the new clothes I had bought for the trip. The tight gowns, for instance, hung uselessly in my closet for my entire stay. By the time I could fit into them again, back in Mao's China, they were not suitable attire.

East Berlin in 1951 was still a city of rubble. Most streets were lined with damaged and dilapidated buildings. Disciplined hard work could be seen everywhere as "volunteer" labour brigades worked on construction projects around the city.

I soon became aware that we were leading a relatively privileged existence in the hotel. For the Germans themselves, many items were rationed, including butter, potatoes, sugar, meat and some clothing. The differences between East and West Berliners were obvious. West Berlin women wore fine nylon stockings; East Berlin women wore thick ones of coarse material that wore out quickly.

Because we lived and worked in the hotel, after a while cabin fever set in. The routine was rigid. I got up, went to the dining room for breakfast, went to the hotel room that functioned as our office to do my typing, back to the dining room for lunch, short nap, more work, back to the dining room for dinner.

In the evenings, Feng and I would take a walk or go to a film.

One of my favourites was a Swedish romance called *The Last Summer*. No doubt it was tame by Swedish standards, but one scene in which a woman swam naked took our breath away. We had never seen nudity on the screen before. Everyone in the delegation saw the film at one time or another, furtively.

The sixty marks we were given for spending money didn't go very far, so Feng and I did a lot more window shopping than buying. A kilo of oranges cost five marks; getting a roll of black-and-white film developed cost more than ten marks.

Many evenings, especially in winter, were spent at the ping-pong table set up in a lounge. Sometimes Feng and I got carried away and an irritated hotel guest would poke his head around the door to point out it was past midnight. Occasionally dance parties were organized, especially at holidays. One New Year's Eve we had a big dinner at the Chinese embassy, and when we got back late to the hotel, most of us were tipsy.

"Hey, let's have a little dance party!" one of the men suggested.

"All that food and drink tonight was exhausting! I'm off to bed!" Feng giggled, and we spun on our heels and headed down the hall to our room. We were already in our pyjamas when a knock came at the door.

"C'mon! It's New Year's Eve! Won't you join us?" yelled Wu, one of our interpreters, through the door. Feng and I amounted to two-thirds of the female component of the delegation, so our absence did put a damper on their dancing party.

"Sorry! We're ready for bed. We don't want to get dressed again," Feng yelled back.

"This is nothing formal, just ourselves. C'mon! Nobody's going to see you," Wu said as he came bursting through the door. He literally dragged the two of us out, down the hall to the ping-pong lounge. So Feng and I, still in our pyjamas, were caught up in the dancing to our small collection of records, mostly German folk music. There still weren't enough women to go around, so some of the men danced with other men.

A few days later, Dai, the Party's representative, called a special meeting. The embassy had instructed him to inform us of new regulations: "No dancing in your pyjamas. And men are not to dance with other men." We never knew how they got wind of our impromptu dance party. On other occasions we got into trouble because of an innocent kindness shown us by a Westerner. There was, for instance, the case of Mr. Silver's chocolate.

Adolf Silver, who worked for the London Export Corporation, was a regular visitor to our office. He acted as a go-between for British companies who were opposed to the Western trade embargo against China. He was an amiable fellow who always brought us chocolates from England. They were the best we had ever had. Then one day the head of the delegation met privately with Mr. Silver and asked him to stop bringing chocolates. Shen had become worried that if word got back to Beijing, it might be construed as bribery.

A few months later, I received permission to ask Mr. Silver for one last favour: to bring me a beginners' book on shorthand. Mr. Silver was delighted to oblige and on his next visit handed me a book-sized package. I ripped off the wrapping paper and found the book I had requested, and, underneath it, a fat chocolate bar almost the size of the book. I was aghast. What if any of the other people in the office had seen? I bit my lower lip as I composed a polite refusal in my head.

"Shhh!" Mr. Silver put his finger to his lips.

"Oh well," I thought and moved my mouth in a soundless "thank you." He left the office with a grin on his face.

A couple of years later, in 1954, Mr. Silver's company was involved in forming the "48 Group of British Traders with China" so called because 48 businessmen attended its founding meeting. The group fought a lonely battle in the West against the trade embargo imposed on communist China, which became even more stringent after China was deemed the aggressor in the 1950-53 Korean War.

On weekends, the East German Ministry of Foreign Trade sometimes organized sightseeing trips for us, but for the most part we were on our own. We often took the U-bahn to the suburbs where we strolled in the woods. One afternoon, a few of us were returning from one of these excursions and were so tired we missed our stop. The subway went hurtling on towards West Berlin. By the time we realized our mistake, it was too late. We had no choice but to get off at the first stop in West Berlin.

We didn't dare venture outside the station, but we did take a quick look around it. The temptation was too great not to have a glimpse at the West. News stands stacked with American magazines and newspapers, chocolate and Coca-Cola; wild advertisements; people walking around chewing gum and whistling. It was all very startling and seemed to me the epitome of the American lifestyle.

I recalled the warnings we had received not to stray into the West. "Remember we have no diplomatic relations with West Germany," Dai had said. "If you land in West Berlin you will be kidnapped and your passport confiscated. Then you could be handed over to the Taiwan authorities."

I was worried that plainclothes police would approach us and demand to see the passports we didn't have with us. We were aware that we stood out: our Chinese faces, our scared-rabbit expressions, our relatively dowdy clothes, the way we pressed close together as we hurried over to the opposite platform to take the train back.

"Walk faster," hissed Wei, one of our interpreters. "Don't look around. Act natural!" The trip from one platform to the other seemed endless. What a relief when we were back on a train heading east.

As our foray into the West had been accidental, we agreed to avoid criticism and keep our mouths shut. But it had been such an exciting adventure that I did whisper it to someone, a young man in our group to whom I had taken a shine. He immediately turned us in, and we were roundly criticized in front of the whole delegation for not reporting it ourselves.

Feng was furious with me. "You idiot! No one would have known! Can't you keep your mouth shut?" She had a point. For weeks afterwards, I felt ashamed before the confederates I had betrayed and guilty before the superiors I had disobeyed.

Despite this infraction, the head of our delegation showed a special interest in my welfare. I took it as a thoughtful superior's concern for a young subordinate when Shen singled me out to take me sightseeing. We were always accompanied on these excursions by his male secretary, Hong. Shen took a lot of pictures of me, bought me presents and sometimes wanted me to be at meetings where my presence was not really needed. I felt flattered.

But Feng saw it differently. Although only a year older than me, she was much more savvy about human behaviour. "Remember, men don't give you things for nothing," she warned me. "Someday he'll make you feel like you owe him something."

I thought she was overreacting. Or maybe she was jealous. "Look here, Feng. He's over forty and I'm only seventeen. He's got a wife and children. He's my superior and a party member. What do you think he could possibly do to me?" The clincher, in my view, was his party membership. That practically guaranteed that he was selfless, upright, noble-minded and completely trustworthy.

"Do what you like but mark my words," Feng said. "I don't like to see you running around with those two."

One Saturday evening, I ran into Shen in the corridor.

"Zhimei, bring me the files you were working on earlier today. I'll be in my room." It was an unusual request, but I did as I was told.

The door to his suite was open when I arrived.

"Close the door," he said. He was sitting on the couch in his pyjamas. In the dimly lit corridor I hadn't noticed that his face was flushed from alcohol.

"Are these the documents you wanted?" I asked.

"Leave them on the desk. Sit down. I want to talk to you." He motioned me toward the couch. I sat as far from him as possible and twisted a handkerchief nervously.

"You're a clever girl, Zhimei," he said, "and I see a lot of potential in you. I want you to be my personal secretary. I'll train you myself."

I was speechless. Feng's "mark my words" echoed in my head. Suddenly, Shen lunged towards me on the couch.

"I like you so much. I've liked you since the first day you walked into my office." He held my hand in a tight grip. "My wife and I don't get along any more. Anyway, she's far away in China and my life here is very hard, very lonely. I think you're the sort of person who likes to help other people." He put his arms around me and drew me towards him. "I think you could help me feel better, don't you?"

"No! No!" I tried to pull free, but his arms were powerful. I wanted to scream, but dared not. In the struggle, two buttons on my blouse popped open. Shen's bloodshot eyes were terrifying; the smell of alcohol on his breath was nauseating. "No! I can't!" I kept saying, and gave him a strong push. Then he got angry.

"Who do you think you are? Ling is prettier than you. If I want her I can have her any time." He was bellowing now and I was worried we could be heard outside the room. Ling was another of our typists and also just a teenager.

"I didn't expect you to be this stubborn," Shen continued. "I thought you'd know how to respond to a special favour. I could help you get ahead. Now you've put yourself in a difficult position and you've only yourself to blame."

I was scared. "May I leave?"

"Yes. But don't mention this to anybody or . . . " He left the threat hanging.

As I turned the doorknob, he barked, "Pull yourself together." I ran my fingers through my hair, buttoned my blouse and left.

Racing back to my room, I passed a delegation member sitting in the lounge. I thought Bao shot me a knowing look, having deduced where I had been. In our small circle, nothing went unnoticed. It was not just curiosity that motivated people to find out everyone else's business, but also a sense of duty. Now Bao would assume I had submitted to my boss's advances and word would get around. He might feel obliged to report what he had seen, although that was tricky when the boss was involved. I felt sullied by the whole experience.

From late 1951 to the middle of 1952, Mao spearheaded a campaign targeting the "three evils": corruption, waste and bureaucracy within the party, government and army. During the campaign, all personal letters we received from China were opened and read by Dai, the party secretary. Some people were asked to read their personal letters aloud to the delegation. The idea was to root out corruption back home, but things of a different nature also came to light. One day, Dai gave me a letter written in English that he wanted translated. It was a love letter to Lu, a married man in the delegation, from his girlfriend in Shanghai.

One man deeply involved in embezzlement was Hong, my boss's secretary. When his activities were revealed in letters Dai intercepted, he was summoned back to China. Police were waiting to handcuff him when he arrived in Beijing. Shen was also called back to be reprimanded for trusting Hong. He was replaced in our office by Tan, who was strict and efficient and, I believe, not given to attacking the young women who worked for him.

Life in Berlin settled into a pleasant, if boring, routine. It was pleasant not to cook or do housework, not to have to squeeze ourselves on to and elbow our way off Beijing's crowded buses. But the longer we stayed, the more monotonous life became. Men who had been away from their wives for a year or two began trying to interest us three young girls in sexual relationships. Others started flirting with the chambermaids, who flirted back. Walking around town we could see why: there were few men in East Berlin after the war.

When our delegation was reorganized into two groups, my

section, which dealt with trade with the West, moved out of the hotel to a residential building near the Chinese embassy. Some time later, our group was amalgamated with an East German company called the China Export Corporation. It was the first place outside China where mainland Chinese and foreigners worked in the same office.

We began socializing with our German colleagues; we went swimming and dancing with them and now felt much less cut off from life in the city. I particularly liked the director of our office from the German side, Frau Hentze. She was in her mid-thirties, nearly twice my age. I admired her competence, her soft-spoken, educated manner and flawless English. I got to know her better a couple of years later when I was assigned to be her interpreter when she visited China in 1955. But our friendship was later to have painful consequences.

I also got on well with one of the German interpreters, Fräulein Hoffmann, an attractive woman with a sunny personality. One day, the head of my section in the office was recalled to China with no warning. Normally people received a few weeks' notice. Whatever Yao had done must have been very serious. Eventually, word got around that he and Fräulein Hoffmann had attempted to elope to Switzerland, but their plan had been discovered. Was their secret betrayed by a Chinese or a German?

Yao was ordered to stay away from the office and get ready to leave. The next morning I saw him in our dormitory building. He walked past me without lifting his head. His characteristic arrogance was gone. Once, I had thrown some files on the floor and stormed out of the office because I couldn't stand his self-important behaviour, his condescending manner with women. Now my dislike of him was replaced by sympathy.

That same afternoon, Fräulein Hoffmann stopped me in the corridor. She took my hand and led me into a small washroom. The pretty young woman looked dreadful now – face pale, eyes swollen.

"I know I can trust you, Zhimei. Would you do me a favour?" Her voice was trembling as she whispered her request. "I won't have a chance to see Yao before he leaves. I'm leaving, too, you know. They're transferring me out. I'll never see him again."

She reached into her skirt pocket and pulled out a small envelope. "Would you give it to him?" She was near tears. I felt so sorry for her.

"Don't worry. I'll give it to him." We left the washroom separately, hoping no one had seen us enter together.

I tossed and turned that night, fighting with my conscience. Should I give the letter to Yao? We had been told to report everything we knew about their relationship to the party secretary so the case could be handled "correctly." But what about the promise I had made to Fräulein Hoffmann? I was sorry I had accepted the letter in the first place. Now I felt trapped.

Finally, I made my decision. It had been drilled into us to place the party's interests above everything else, including friendships and personal lives. I was thirteen when the communists took over in Beijing; now, at eighteen, I sincerely believed it was wrong to hide anything from the party. I was also worried that I would be viewed as an accomplice if the letter was discovered. Because of my "bad" family background, I thought the punishment might be severe for even this relatively minor act of disloyalty.

The next morning, after a sleepless night, I handed the letter to the party secretary. I explained what had happened and asked *him* to pass it on to Yao. I felt great relief, and guilt. I was ashamed when I saw Fräulein Hoffmann the next morning. Her beloved had received her farewell letter, or so she thought. She flashed me a smile of gratitude.

Our German colleagues could not understand why the Chinese were trying to stop the marriage. To them, it seemed a heartwarming symbol of internationalism and fraternal relations between two socialist countries, and hardly the scandalous breach of discipline it was treated as.

Frau Haupt, a woman in her sixties who had lost her husband and son in the Second World War, was particularly upset. She shook her head sadly: "Why separate such an ideal couple? I just can't understand it." A member of the East German Communist Party, she accepted all our other policies and decisions except that one.

Yao left Berlin without being given a chance to say goodbye to Fräulein Hoffmann. He sent her a postcard from Moscow on his way home, but she was never given it. Because of Yao's attempted defection to Switzerland, our boss, Tan, was also recalled to China. We were going through bosses at the rate of one a year.

The next boss came charging on to the scene with a campaign of his own invention. He was determined to raise our level of political consciousness. We were all to make a public "evaluation" of our past conduct, measuring ourselves against the high standards of discipline set by the party.

I spent two days preparing my presentation, earnestly trying to give a balanced picture of myself, complete with strengths and shortcomings. I told my colleagues I considered myself hardworking, disciplined and loyal to the party. On the other hand, I had not devoted enough time to reading political books, nor had I applied to join the Communist Youth League. But this, I stressed, was my most cherished future ambition. I was pleased with my spiel, convinced I had given an honest self-appraisal.

"I think there's something she hasn't mentioned," said a senior comrade, rising to his feet. "And it's important to point it out to her. Her relations with the German colleagues are far too close. If we had placed stricter rules on this before, other comrades wouldn't have committed the mistakes they did."

Before I had a chance to recover from the shock of this intervention, another comrade got up to elaborate.

"At the dance last week, Zhimei danced much too much with a German man. Some of us noticed that he held her so tightly that their faces were almost touching. It was very improper."

What could I say in my defence? The man did dance many times with me. He did hold me tightly. But I had never expected the others to be so observant or to take it so seriously.

This was the first behavioral black mark in my dossier, which grew to be very thick over time. Berlin was my first and last posting abroad. I was recalled to Beijing in early 1954 and it was years before I understood the reason: my father had just been classified a counter-revolutionary because of his work in Japanese-controlled offices during the occupation. On my way back to China, I passed through Moscow and made a return visit to Red Square, where Stalin's embalmed corpse now lay beside Lenin's.

My parents were getting ready for bed when I arrived home. My family all looked much the same as two years earlier, but our house looked completely different. The ceiling seemed lower, the lights dimmer, the walls filthier. And it was very cold. The one coal stove couldn't heat the four rooms. I had seen a bit of the outside world and had lived in conditions better than this. The ambivalence I felt on my return never completely vanished.

A few months after my return, an "election" was held at which citizens were invited to endorse the first National People's Congress choice of Mao Zedong as party chairman and, among other leaders, Deng Xiaoping as a vice-premier of the State Council. Reporters covering the poll in my parents' neighbourhood were impressed by my mother's silver-grey hair, and the photographs of her that appeared in newspapers were intended to show the enthusiasm of older people in the voting. Had they known that her husband was a "counter-revolutionary," deprived of the right to vote, they might have thought twice about choosing her as a model elderly voter.

After Berlin, I was assigned to the translation department of the China National Import/Export Corporation. I had two plans in mind. One was to go to college and get some professional training and the other was to join the Communist Youth League; not being a league member was a clear sign of political backwardness. On

July 1, 1954, at a meeting held to mark the 33rd anniversary of the party's founding, I publicly declared my resolve to become a youth league member. But membership was not automatic; you had to prove your loyalty.

I started to write critically about myself, recounting my family background and current attitude toward it. I concluded that not much in my life or about my family was politically correct. Even though my father was unemployed and my mother a seamstress, we were still bourgeois. I had come to accept that it was ideas and outlook that counted.

About my father, I wrote: "He worked in Japanese-controlled offices. He was the scum of the nation, devoid of any national dignity."

About my mother: "She was a mahjong addict and lived an extravagant lifestyle. Did working people have time to play mahjong? Only bourgeois types like my mother, who were waited on hand and foot, had the time and money to waste on mahjong."

About myself: "I attended a missionary school. Being educated by foreigners poisoned my mind and my soul. My family background and foreign education led me into a bourgeois lifestyle. I went to dance halls when I was fifteen and I liked to sing Western popular songs. I liked to dress nicely and to have admirers. Now I must remold myself thoroughly."

I churned out page after page of this kind of self-criticism, but it was not enough to earn me youth league membership. I had not yet proved my loyalty.

In 1955, a nationwide campaign was launched to "eliminate reactionaries." Our department's initial target was an older man named Yang who had worked for a foreign company before Liberation and whose family was Protestant. We were told to recall whether we had ever heard him say anything against the party or socialist system, or try to corrupt young people's minds with his bourgeois ideas. I remembered one incident. It was a Sunday, and Yang and his family had stopped by our house on their way to church. He had a book in his hand, and I asked what it was.

"This is my Marxism," he laughed, and held the New Testament up for me to see.

A meeting was called at work and we were all, in turn, told to repeat things that Yang had said to us. I came under particular pressure because he and I had often been seen chatting, practising our English together. All I could think of to recount was his joke about his Bible, which did not strike me as being a particularly damaging revelation. After all, some churches were still allowed to operate in those days.

The magnitude of what I had done didn't register until the day a notice went up announcing Yang's fate. I happened to be standing beside him as we both read it for the first time. He was to be expelled from work. In a system in which all jobs were assigned by the state, this meant he would never work again.

I was as stunned as he was. In addition to his past offenses, little anecdotes such as the one I had related were used to concoct a "current crime" and brand him a reactionary. I didn't have the courage to look him in the face. I imagined him saying "Are you happy now?" – words he never did say, but which haunted me for a long time afterward. His life was ruined and I got my league membership because I had stood the test.

My betrayal of Yang did not sit right with my conscience. Like most other young people in the early years after Liberation I was eager to show my patriotism. Backward, impoverished China had stood up, and we were only too willing to do our part to help build a new order. We trusted the party leaders who had made the revolution and so did the things we were told to do.

I felt badly about my role in Yang's downfall, but was still a long way from conscious recognition of why it made me uncomfortable. Over the years, after each political campaign, a painful realization came into focus more clearly for me. Human behaviour and relationships were deteriorating in China. It was sickening to see wives informing on husbands, children turning in their parents and students squealing on teachers. The campaigns bred fear and compliance; anybody could turn informer overnight.

And so it should have come as little surprise to see the nation run amok during the Cultural Revolution a decade later. Millions were killed, and millions of other lives destroyed. But the seeds had been embedded years before in a code of behaviour sanctioned by the party in which betrayal and revenge had become part of a new morality. It was dehumanizing. Before becoming targets ourselves, many of us had betrayed someone else. We were becoming a nation of victims and victimizers.

Chapter Five

FOUR PESTS AND TWO MEN

Soon after I became a youth league member, I got permission to take an advanced course in international trade. I now had two badges shining on my chest: youth league membership and attendance at the prestigious Institute of Foreign Trade. I was on the way up. After finishing the course, I was transferred to work in the China National Chemical Import/Export Corporation.

The Anti-Rightist Movement, begun in June 1957, was in full swing. It had been launched to crack down on critics who had come forward in the earlier Hundred Flowers campaign. For about a year, intellectuals had been encouraged to speak their minds. Now they were being punished for the things they had said.

I had a boyfriend, an intelligent young engineer who worked in a government office but whose family background was even worse than my own. Xian's father, a Shanghai capitalist, had been executed soon after Liberation. As I walked into my office one afternoon, my colleagues' conversation stopped. I pretended not to have noticed, but the abrupt silence was ominous.

A woman whose husband worked in Xian's office made a point of leaving with me at the end of the day. On our way to the bus stop, she said quietly: "Do you know what's happened to Xian? My husband told me last night that he's an extreme rightist. His mistakes are serious and he's being openly criticized now."

That explained Xian's strange behaviour recently. He had

become absent-minded and moody, sighing more than he talked.

"What are his mistakes?"

"Once when he and some colleagues were discussing an engineering problem, the party secretary walked by and offered some advice. After he left, Xian snorted and said: 'What does he know about engineering, anyway?' "

The party secretary was not, in fact, a trained engineer. But if you suggested a party boss was not equipped to offer you technical advice in your field, it was as if you were openly questioning the party's authority to lead the country.

"Another time, at a meeting in which a Soviet engineering project was being held up as a model, Xian said during the discussion period that Chinese conditions were different in some respects. 'Must we blindly copy everything Soviet? Shouldn't we adapt things to our own situation?' " Such a suggestion was interpreted as an attack on the special fraternal relationship between the two countries.

"You must decide what to do now," she said. That much was obvious. Anyone linked to a rightist, by family ties or friendship, had to dissociate themselves or share the stigma. I had a hard time that evening. I knew I should stop seeing Xian, and I also knew that would not be enough. If I didn't draw a clear line between myself and a class enemy, it would be my downfall, too.

An extreme rightist was defined as a person with a deep hatred for the state, a counter-revolutionary to the marrow of his bones. They would be looking for plenty of "evidence" to make the label stick. I would have to report anything I had ever heard Xian say against the party or communist system.

I went to see a cousin of Xian's whom I knew well. The cousin showed me the letter he himself had already handed in: "Xian has become a class enemy, and I hate him. I will draw a sharp line between us. The party's interests are more important than anything else." It was a stilted, rather unbelievable letter, but it wasn't important whether he meant it or not. It was the gesture that counted.

Keeping one's political reputation in order was more important than one's personal life. If branded by the party, you lost your job, were shunned by your friends and became a serious liability to your entire extended family. I tried to remember things Xian had said in past conversations that might be "incorrect." There was nothing very damaging in the report I handed in but, again, it was the gesture that counted. I promised to stop seeing him.

Soon afterwards, I kept a date with him. He still knew nothing of my decision, or even that I was aware of his political problems. We met on a street corner and he immediately handed me a package: "My mother had these shoes made for you in Shanghai." The shoes were stylish and made of fine black leather. Then Xian popped the question: "My mother asked me whether we're going to get married."

"The shoes are beautiful. Please thank her for me." I was alarmed at this turn of events and deliberately avoided the second topic. We walked silently to a nearby restaurant.

"I like the romantic atmosphere here," Xian said as we slid into a booth. The restaurant served Japanese food, and Xian ordered sukiyaki for two and a bottle of sake.

"You haven't answered my question," he said, after filling our sake cups. There was a painful silence as I struggled to find the words.

Finally, I spoke: "I don't think I can continue seeing you."

It had come as a surprise. He said nothing for several minutes, draining one sake cup and then another. Then he said sadly: "I know I've ruined my life and shattered my dreams. But I thought at least that I still had you." He poured himself a third sake, and then pulled a well-thumbed notebook from his jacket pocket. "Would you do something for me and read this? There might not be another chance."

It was his diary. I read it while he continued drinking, cup after cup of sake. Soon the bottle was empty and he ordered another. I had never seen him drink like this before.

His journal contained a moving day-by-day account of our relationship: the day we met, the night we first went dancing, how he had described me to his mother, how he had missed me when he was away on business, how jealous he was of other men around me. His writing was vivid and full of emotion.

I started to cry as I turned the pages. I had always thought him a rather arrogant, macho type and had deliberately kept my emotional distance. I thought I meant as little to him, but I was wrong. He reached for my hand and I looked up from my reading.

"I know I have no right to ask you for anything." The sake was beginning to slur his speech. "But could you wait for me?"

"Let's not talk about the future." I pulled my hand back. "It's too uncertain. Who knows where they'll send you? Who knows how many years you'll be in a labour camp? I'm sorry. I can't promise you anything."

A strand of hair swung loosely on his forehead. He was a tall, handsome man with delicate features, but now his face, set alight by the sake, shone a brilliant red.

"Don't drink any more. Let's go."

"No, let me drink. I want to forget. I want to die." He started to sob. I was nervous. I asked the waitress for a wet towel to wipe his face.

"Leave me alone," he said, swatting at my hand as I tried to wipe his face. Other customers began to stare. Finally he agreed to leave, but by then he couldn't stand up straight. He wobbled forward and threw up. The waitress was nice and didn't complain. She helped me clean up the mess.

Soon afterwards, Xian was sent to a remote village, where he spent many years working in the paddy fields. We never saw each other again.

The following year, the mood of accusation and anti-intellectualism in the country stirred up by the Anti-Rightist Movement still prevailed when Mao launched the Great Leap Forward. The goal was to overcome economic backwardness through sheer force of will. If everyone put their minds to it, China could speed development to a dizzying pace.

Everyone was to help build and operate backyard steel furnaces. These primitive smelters were supposed to crank out steel in sufficient quantity that China's output would overtake Britain's and catch up with the United States' in twenty years.

Peasants marched about in the countryside waving banners and clashing cymbals, turning out poor-quality pig-iron and neglecting their fields. Despite a reduced harvest, grain exports to the Soviet Union were increased in 1959 in exchange for machinery to promote heavy industry. It was the prelude to a devastating famine that would kill an estimated twenty million people or more.

In urban areas, factories, schools and households all heeded the call to surrender whatever they had that could be melted down to produce steel: pots and woks, coal stoves, door knobs; anything, in fact, whether decorative or useful, that was made of iron or steel. Mostly people contributed pots and pans, and these soon disappeared from kitchens and turned up on the rationed list. We were also encouraged to hand over whatever we had that could keep the smelters blazing. My mother even gave up her chopping board, a precious slab of wood of a sort that was no longer available in stores.

Secondary campaigns were waged against the backdrop of the struggle for rapid industrialization. The campaign to clean up infested cities became a national passion in the summer of 1958. As the capital, Beijing was expected to set an example for the country. "Away with the four pests!" was the slogan of the day.

Sparrows, rats, flies and mosquitoes helped me sail through my next test of loyalty to the party. My particular forte was fly-swatting: I set and surpassed astonishing personal quotas. Pests were plentiful; they ate our food and sucked our blood, so it wasn't hard to mobilize a willing people's army of exterminators. Sacrificing leisure time, even going without the noon nap, seemed a small price to pay to defeat these carriers of disease.

Sparrows were targeted because they consumed precious grain. The birds were not simply poisoned or shot from the sky; they were tortured to death. People clambered on to the roofs of houses, and stood there for hours on end beating drums and gongs, bellowing and waving banners. The sparrows, terrified by the din, would take one look at the frenzy and refuse to land anywhere near it. They circled for as long as they could and finally plummeted to the earth, exhausted. Suddenly sparrows appeared on restaurant menus as never before. Deep-fried, crispy head and all, they were very tasty.

One afternoon, a meeting at my office with the Czechoslovakian commercial attaché was interrupted by a great clashing of gongs coming from the roof. We could barely hear each other in the pandemonium. The diplomat leaned over and yelled in my ear: "What's the holiday?"

"They're just chasing sparrows," I bellowed back.

He looked sceptical. "Do you really think you can get rid of all the sparrows this way?"

"People wouldn't be doing it if it didn't work," I said with, I hoped, a note of conviction. I wasn't at all sure of the truth of that, but in those days I was afraid to whisper, let alone shout, anything that strayed from the party line.

"And is it such a good idea to kill the birds in the first place?" the diplomat yelled above the din.

He had a point. China's bird population had taken a nosedive, and the insects they normally ate were returning to feast on the crops. In recognition of this problem, sparrows were taken off the list of pests in 1960 and replaced by bedbugs.

While my own expertise at felling sparrows was pretty average, flies were another matter. We had a competition on at work to see who could kill the most, and the daily tally was tacked up on the office wall. The party secretary opened departmental meetings with a report on the body count.

"Kang killed the most flies this week – 3,256." (He paused to lead

85

the applause.) "Her serious attitude toward the campaign deserves praise. I hope the rest of you follow her example and go on to set even higher records."

"How on earth did she manage that?" I wondered. I didn't think I could swat that many flies even if I did nothing but hunt them all day long. I asked her her secret.

"Come with me after lunch," she whispered.

It was a steamy July day but I skipped my nap and followed Kang to a back alley. Even before it came into view, my nose had detected her secret. A huge mound of vegetables lay rotting in the summer heat. The stench was appalling – and the flies! I couldn't believe our luck. They were big ones, blowflies made sluggish by the hot sun. You had only to bat your flyswatter back and forth and they fell at your feet.

"One, two, three . . . 50 . . . 100 . . . . I can't keep track!" I yelled in delight. "How many have you killed?"

I turned toward Kang at the other end of the dump. She was lost in concentration, a petite silhouette in constant motion against a blazing sun. I stopped to admire her expert jig. She held a flyswatter with one hand and a handkerchief over her nose with the other. Her skirt swung furiously as she danced a frenetic, irregular step. She was trying to avoid stomping on rotten tomatoes and causing them to spurt their juice on to her skirt. My own white skirt was now covered in bright red stains.

Kang and I went regularly together to the back alley during our two-hour lunch breaks. Because we were missing our midday naps, many of us found it hard to concentrate on work in the afternoon and especially hard to keep awake at political meetings.

But my fly-swatting scores were soaring. We were responsible for reporting our own tally, and were so disciplined it never occurred to us to inflate the count. In any case, I wouldn't have had the nerve to make up the kind of real figures I began chalking up after Kang shared her garbage dump with me.

Eventually the whole thing began to bother me. Why was the

garbage left strewn about in the first place, allowed to become such a splendid breeding ground? We arrived to kill the flies and set our records. Then more garbage was dumped, more flies made plump, more lunch-hours spent killing them. What kind of crazy cycle was this? Why not put the same effort into improving garbage disposal?

I was sharing a room with a colleague in the women's dormitory at my work unit. We weren't bothered by rats, because it was a new building. But my family's courtyard house was more than 100 years old and badly infested. When we first moved to the place I was often wakened by the wailing of a cat in heat or rats on their nightly rounds. My ears would follow the tapping of feet on the wood floors as a rat scurried about its business.

During the campaign, every family was supposed to set out rat-traps. Ours simply acted as a food-dispenser until a neighbour advised: "Bait the trap with a piece of pork crackling; it's greasy, smells good, but is difficult to chew off. Whatever you do, don't put cooked meat on the hook, that's too easy for the rat to make off with."

Rat poison was distributed to every household. We were meant to press it into the holes in the floorboards. Hua had a practical mind: she worried that if the rats died in their holes, the smell of their decay would fill our house and, of more concern, an epidemic would follow. So we were careful to spread the powder along the floorboards, but not inside the holes, hoping to avoid fatalities between the walls.

It was against the backdrop of the four pests campaign that I met two men, almost simultaneously. One was Zhou, a university lecturer who had spent many years in the United States studying for a degree in architecture, and who had returned to China a couple of years earlier. His sister worked in my office and she introduced us. We went out dancing a few times and had great fun. He was a knowledgeable, interesting companion.

The other was vice-secretary of the youth league section at my work unit. Wang had enlisted in the army from his home town, Tangshan, the city northeast of Beijing that was virtually levelled by an earthquake in 1976. To join the People's Liberation Army was many boys' dream. The army was the height of revolutionary respectability, lauded in novels, films and plays. It brought great honour on a household to have a family member in the army. A red banner with the words "Honoured Family" could be hung over the door.

Such a banner graced our landlady's doorway because her daughter worked for the army's August First Film Company. She no longer mentioned her landowner family background, which had been her pride in earlier days. Now she reminded her neighbours of the privileges an Honoured Family enjoyed. She would get excited about any perk: "I've been given free tickets to see a war film!" On national holidays, local cadres would pay the family a visit, which implied special concern. The Honoured Family sign saved that house from being ransacked when Red Guards swept through our courtyard during the Cultural Revolution.

Soon after he enlisted, Wang was sent to the Military Foreign Languages Institute to learn Japanese. Four years later, graduation from the course marked the end of his army career. It had not been his choice to transfer to civilian work, but he was deemed unfit to work in the army because before Liberation a distant uncle had belonged to a reactionary group allied to the Kuomintang.

"Nobody would have learned of my uncle's past affiliation if I had not confessed it," Wang said. "Actually this uncle of mine was only a nominal member; he had no idea of the nature of the group. Times were hard and he'd been desperate for a job. Before the group had a chance to train him for anything, the communists had liberated the country. He had done no harm."

"Then why did you confess something that had no real meaning but which could only bring trouble for yourself and your family?" I asked.

"Nothing should be hidden from the party," he said, sounding, as he often did, like a slogan. As a result of his confession, Wang was deemed to have "complicated social connections." Those words in one's personnel file were the kiss of death for certain jobs. So, too "complicated" for the army, he was assigned to my work unit.

Wang often went about in his old army uniform. I found the plainness of the look appealing. He was tall and athletic and spoke eloquently at meetings. But I was most impressed by his writing. Once he went, with thousands of others, to help build the Ming Tomb reservoir outside Beijing. His letters to me from there were richly descriptive, even poetic. I pored over each of the lines and then looked between them for a hint of something romantic, but there was none of that to be found. Then I felt guilty for having undertaken the search, evidence of my unhealthy, petit-bourgeois sentimentalism.

I couldn't make up my mind between the two men – between Zhou and his sense of fun, and Wang and his sense of duty. But I had to choose, and fast. If a man and woman were often seen in public together, it was assumed they would marry. How could I continue to be seen with two men? It was an untenable situation, and long before I had had a chance to get to know either man very well, I had to choose.

I decided to ask Ni, the youth league secretary, for advice. I knew nothing should be hidden from the party and its youth branch, but I had great difficulty broaching this subject. I was not used to talking about personal matters, even with my sisters.

Ni's office was as neat and tidy as the man himself. I sat opposite him across a spotless desk and began to stammer out the reason for my visit: "I . . . I have a practical problem." I told Ni that I had met two men and needed the league's help in deciding between them.

He hesitated before replying. "I'm glad you have a strong sense of party loyalty. As this is a purely personal affair, I can't tell you what to do. But I can advise you to weigh the political considerations very carefully."

I thanked him and left, but I was still puzzled. How was I to go about weighing political considerations? I decided to work out a list: Zhou was "A"; Wang was "B".

Family origin:	A	bourgeois
	B	middle-peasant
Political affiliation:	A	non-party person
	B	youth league member and candidate for party membership
Education:	A	U.S. education
	B	Military Foreign Languages Institute
Social status:	A	bourgeois intellectual
	B	proletarian intellectual

The list went on, comparing differences in their lifestyles, interests, tastes and, of course, political attitudes. Once I had spelled it all out in list form, I could see that I was leaning toward "B" as the sensible choice. I thought that by marrying into a better political and family background, I could escape the stigma of my own background and so could my children.

Political activity filled our lives during the Great Leap Forward. Sunday, our one day off, was devoted to cleaning our office and dormitory rooms. Wang often came to help me with the windows, which I hated doing. In the evenings, we would help set up exhibitions on the achievements of the Great Leap Forward; during our lunch breaks, we swatted flies.

Then there were the mass excursions to building sites around Beijing for week-long stints of voluntary manual labour. The work was voluntary only in the sense that it was unpaid. The Ming Tombs reservoir and Beijing's "ten major buildings," including the Great Hall of the People on Tiananmen Square, were all built during this period, largely by unskilled labour. It was considered a great honour to be involved in the construction of such important buildings, especially the ones around Tiananmen. If you were lucky enough to be conscripted to work on those buildings, it was a sign you were really trusted. Class enemies, potential saboteurs, did not get those assignments.

In all these activities, Wang shone. He was a model worker and skilled propagandist. He showed me the letters of praise he had received from the site officials, and I felt tremendously proud of him. In my eyes he was the very embodiment of the new revolutionary man. Could I, by association, become the new revolutionary woman?

I politely distanced myself from the architecture professor and continued dating Wang. We went to films, took walks together after work. He was attentive and considerate. Amid the food shortages of the Great Leap, Wang rose at dawn to fetch me the best food available in the canteen. We were living in the dormitories for single men and women, and every morning when I arrived at work, I found breakfast waiting for me on my desk. Again, at noon, he was first in line at the canteen, so that I would have the best dishes. I was well taken care of.

"You're so lucky!" said my roommate, a daycare worker. She thought I had the best catch.

But one of my colleagues was blunt about her view. "Wang is a very nice person and he has many good qualities. But a nice person isn't necessarily compatible with you in the long run. You're from totally different backgrounds, and the differences will start to matter sooner or later. If I were you, I'd rely more on my head in this matter than my feelings."

I knew there was something to what she said. I had already felt the strain of the incompatibility between us in practically all spheres other than politics and work: ballroom dancing, for instance. It was popular in China both before Liberation and into the 1950s. I loved it so much that for years I never missed one of the free weekly dances organized at our work unit.

Wang didn't dance. He sat on the sidelines and watched while I waltzed away with other partners. But because I was spoken for, colleagues who used to be my regular dance partners were now reluctant to ask me. I became a wallflower, looking on enviously as other young couples moved gracefully around the dance floor. Eventually I stopped going to the dances altogether. I liked going to movies and discussing them afterwards. Wang enjoyed seeing films, too, but later he would agree instantly with whatever I said and never venture an opinion of his own.

I was unimpressed; didn't he have his own ideas? I wanted to be loved and cared for, but the ways he found to express that – waiting on me hand and foot, agreeing with me up and down, popping into my office with irritating frequency – were not what I had in mind. And I wished he could talk about things that were a bit more interesting than his life in the army. When we were out with his army friends, I felt totally out of place.

I knew my mother didn't like the sound of him, but eventually it came time to take Wang home for inspection. I briefed him carefully. He must not, for instance, arrive empty-handed on the first visit. So we bought some wine and cakes on our way to my parents' house.

When I introduced him to my parents, Wang was tense, trying hard to be polite. As is usual when addressing men and women one's parents' age, he called them aunt and uncle. But oh, disaster! Barely through the door and his foot was already in his mouth. He had chosen the words for aunt and uncle that are heard in the countryside, terms peasants would use among themselves. Educated city people would never use those words. Things were off to a bad start.

It was a sweltering midsummer day. The front door and a back window were thrown open, but still there was no cross-breeze. We crowded around the table in my parents' cramped quarters. My father, who did most of the cooking, brought in steaming dishes of food until the small table was laden.

Suddenly, I watched in horror as Wang rolled up his army pants for extra ventilation. I couldn't believe my eyes as he started scratching his legs nervously while my mother pressed him for information about his family. I had worried for weeks about what sort of first impression he would make, and here he was acting as if he was squatting with his buddies in boot camp. I could barely restrain myself from jumping up and yanking his trouser legs back down.

What a contrast to visiting my parents the year before with my "rightist" boyfriend, Xian. From an upper-class Shanghai family, his refined manners were bred in the bone. He had been taught never to raise his voice in conversation, to sit up straight when visiting, to avoid inappropriate topics when talking with the elderly and to be fastidious about table manners. Of course, on the subject of behaviour, Xian could also be a pain in the neck. Once, as we were waiting for a bus after a late movie, I leaned sleepily against the bus-stop. "Women don't stand that way," he upbraided me. "It's not graceful."

I felt torn as I watched Wang trying hard with my parents. He was basically a good man, certainly a fine comrade, and I was annoyed at myself for caring about things that one part of me considered trivial.

My mother scrutinized him from head to toe. "Eat, eat," she said as she piled more food into his bowl, but there was no genuine look of welcome on her face. My father was always nice and receptive to anyone I brought home. "I don't care who you choose, just as long as you're happy," he said.

"Wang looks like a northerner to me," my mother said after he left. When I confirmed her suspicion, she snorted. "I think you should choose a southerner. Northerners don't have the same habits as us." It was a clear reference to Wang's gaffes.

Soon after that visit, Wang and I had our picture taken. Few people had cameras in those days, but city-dwellers liked to go to a portrait studio to record important events, especially marriage. We both liked the way we looked in the picture: cheerful, and neat and tidy in our freshly pressed white shirts. Wang began distributing the picture widely. He sent it to his family in Tangshan, to friends in the army. He even handed it around to colleagues at work. This was not a casual gesture, but a clear statement of intent. I wasn't at all sure I was ready.

Privacy was virtually non-existent; he had his roommate and I had mine. Even when one of our roommates was out, anyone might pop into the room before we had a chance to answer their light tap on the door. We were restricted to holding hands in darkened cinemas. Eventually, an opportunity did present itself when my roommate announced she was going away one weekend. Wang and I brought some food to my room and ate a meal together. It was the first time we had had a chance to eat alone, out of public view. We whispered and walked about on tiptoe. As darkness fell, we decided not to switch on the light, hoping no one would suspect I was in. We locked the door from the inside.

We started to fondle each other and to struggle awkwardly out of pieces of clothing until we were both undressed. We glanced furtively at each other in the near darkness and then, suddenly scared, broke apart. We stopped touching and our conversation turned to mundane subjects. We sat in the dark for a while and then quietly slipped back into our clothes. Was it a sense of morality, or fear of being discovered, or simply embarrassment that kept us from doing more? In any case, because we had gone that far, I knew there was no backing out.

A few days later, Wang announced he had talked to the party secretary at work and our relationship had received official approval. "I think we should join our lives together," he said.

I said not a word, just looked at him and nodded. In this way, awkward and unsmiling, we pledged our troth.

I was disappointed. This is not how I had imagined a marriage proposal. I had thought I might experience a little surge of feeling for the man when he asked me.

"I have something for you," Wang then said. With evident

embarrassment, he handed me a book with its cover papered over. I opened it to the title page: *Facts about Sex.*

"This book is difficult to get," Wang whispered. He had turned bright red. "You should read it, but be careful not to let your roommate see you have it."

I had no idea such a book existed. For the next few nights I read it voraciously, my back turned to my roommate, careful to tuck it under the mattress before sleeping. My parents and older sisters had told me nothing about sex; the nuns at Sacred Heart were equally unforthcoming.

The book's descriptions of the reproductive organs and conception were matter-of-fact biology, but the rest was pure moralizing. Having more than one orgasm was inadvisable because it tired you out. Masturbation was unhealthy from both a physical and moral standpoint. Sex was to be avoided during menstruation.

Love-making was not a spontaneous thing, but was to be guided by certain rules. The text recommended a healthy sexual frequency of two or three times a week.

The book stressed that the glue keeping marriages together was not sex but revolutionary camaraderie. Given that this was the only advice on the subject I had ever received, I took it all very seriously.

My mother wasn't a bit thrilled about me getting married. She thought Wang was nothing special. "You're only twenty-three, far too young to be getting married. You'd do better to wait until you're thirty-five. I would have done a lot of things if I hadn't been tied down with so many children."

My mother believed she was a strong woman, meant to have a career like a man, and so was I. "When you were a child, a friend said, 'That girl of yours will grow up to be a lion.' And I believe it. There are lots of things you could go on to do without a man."

"But Ma," I protested, "if I'm still single after I'm twenty-five, I'll be called an old maid. I don't want to become some kind of weird spinster."

And so, in October 1958, I was married. Preparations for marriage were simple in those days. Extravagance was disdained. We bought sheets and some basic things for the kitchen. But my mother did have two brocade jackets made for me, despite her disapproval of the entire event. "You can't wear old clothes on your wedding day! Wear the rose jacket; it'll bring good luck."

"We need two rings, symbols of our union," I suggested to Wang. He never disagreed with anything I said, so off we went to a jewelry store and bought two 14-karat gold bands. I put mine on right away and he put his in his pocket. He never did wear it. In those days it was considered bourgeois to wear a ring.

The next thing was to get our marriage licence, imprinted with our names and ages, and with the characters "Revolutionary Companions" embossed in bold. A lot of couples had their marriage licences framed and put on proud display in their homes alongside wedding pictures. Ours never showed up on the wall.

It was after dusk when we left the marriage bureau, nervously clutching the piece of paper that made us revolutionary companions. Neither of us said a word. I felt wretched, and tears began streaming down my cheeks.

"What's wrong?" Wang asked. He thought I was overexcited and tried to comfort me. "It's OK, really. All women are like this. They feel sad when they have to leave their parents. But we'll start a happy life together."

We walked to a nearby restaurant, where the tables were crowded up against one another. Normally neither of us drank, but on this occasion we ordered two glasses of red wine to toast our future. When the wine arrived, I held up my glass to his. Our eyes met, and I couldn't hold back the tears. I wasn't in love. Why had I done this, to myself and to him?

Chapter Six

MY FIRST REVOLUTIONARY COMPANION

Although legally registered as man and wife, Wang and I continued to live separately in our dormitories. To apply for a room as a married couple, you had to show your marriage certificate and then wait until space was available. In January 1959, three months after our marriage, a small room in a three-room apartment became vacant. The two other rooms were occupied by the head of the personnel department and his family.

The day we were to move into our new room, a wedding ceremony was held in the big, drafty canteen at work. Teacups and plates of candies, sunflower and watermelon seeds were placed at intervals along tables arranged in a U-shape. Amid the shortages of the Great Leap Forward, we had started buying candy several months beforehand. Good-quality candy was rare, but when it did appear, we snapped up our small ration.

The ceremony was for two couples. Both grooms wore their blue Mao jackets. I wore my rose silk brocade jacket and the other bride wore one in azure silk. Party secretary Zhu, acting as master of ceremonies, sat at the table in the middle of the U, beneath a portrait of Mao. My mother was the only parent present of any of the four "revolutionary companions" being honoured, and I could tell she looked askance at the proceedings. My father had simply stayed home. When my sisters Mei and Hua were married, he had given them away in lavish Western-style weddings, complete with wedding gown and flower girls, champagne and a sumptuous feast.

Those ceremonies were held in cheerfully decorated halls rented for the occasion in fancy hotels. A political meeting in a drab work-unit canteen was not his idea of a wedding.

"You young people are so lucky," secretary Zhu began. "I got married in the war-torn years before Liberation when life was really difficult. We had hardly anything and certainly there was no chance of having a nice ceremony like this. My wife and I just put our two bedrolls together and that was it."

Zhu was following the normal script that opened and closed virtually any meeting – "recall past suffering and reflect on the source of present happiness." That part came next.

"At times like this," he continued, "you should remember the goodness, the kindness of the party, without which today's celebration would not have been possible. And you should be grateful to the party for teaching you that the most important bond holding two people together in a marriage is a shared goal. The party has provided you with those shared revolutionary goals. Now, let's ask our happy couples to tell us how they met and came to decide that they wanted to join their lives together."

This was the part I dreaded. You had to stand up in front of the thirty assembled guests, mostly colleagues you were not particularly close to. You had to shape your personal experience into a revolutionary fable for everyone's edification.

The other couple were older than us, so they went first. The audience spared the bride because she was from another work unit and was shy about talking in front of strangers. So our colleague, the groom, spoke for both of them. He recounted how they had met and were attracted to each other because they were both from the south. This initial attraction deepened over time, he said, as they realized they also shared much more: a desire to work tirelessly for the new China.

As he sat down, everyone clapped and the party secretary sat at the front beaming. The groom was a candidate for party membership and his spiel was made to order.

Then it was our turn. I hated speaking in public, but there was no escaping it this time. I stood up, wriggling my hands nervously. The guests were cracking sunflower seeds, spitting the shells on to the white tablecloth and looking at me expectantly.

"We're different from the other couple," I began and then stopped. What had I meant to say after that? I drew a blank.

"Tell us what's different," someone in the audience piped up as my long silence became awkward.

"Well, what I meant was that Wang and I both work here. Everybody knows how we met and how often we see each other and things like that. I mean, you all see us together every day here in the canteen. There's really nothing I can tell you that you don't already know."

I sat down. The audience, feeling cheated, did not applaud. They cracked sunflower seeds and glowered at me. They had expected to be told a story, and I had merely spoken the banal truth. I really couldn't think of how to weave our story into something uplifting or heartwarming.

Wang, for his part, tried to recover the situation. "Zhimei and I met fourteen months ago. It didn't take us long to realize how much we have in common. She's a hard-working comrade with a serious attitude towards her political life. I think we share these qualities and find them attractive in each other." This was more like it. Heads nodded in approval around the table.

"We are entering into a marriage," Wang continued, "based on the granite foundation of shared progressive values, revolutionary optimism and fervent desire to serve the party. Our decision to marry stemmed from a realization that as man and wife we'll have even more to contribute to society. We're both eager to work for the new China in whatever way we can."

After the applause died down, secretary Zhu turned to my mother and asked if she would like to say a few words. My mother, embarrassed, lowered her head and flapped her hand around to signal "no." She liked public speaking about as much as I did.

The two couples made deep bows to Mao's portrait, to Zhu (as the party's representative), and to each other. To cap off the ceremony, Zhu led the wedding party in a song, "Socialism is Good": ". . . The imperialists have fled with their tails between their legs/There is unity among the people/And socialist construction is booming."

After the ceremony, family members and friends were invited to visit our new room, which was the normal practice. Tiny as the room was, we were pleased to get it at all. We could have languished much longer on the waiting list. The room was just big enough to hold a double bed, writing table, chair and chest of drawers, with little space in between. The only decorative touch was a bust of Chairman Mao on the writing table.

We had to entertain our guests in shifts because no more than six people could squeeze into the room at once; one group would retreat to allow another to enter. The bed, with its new red silk quilt, was too pretty to sit on, so visitors stood around it, wedged in between the furniture. We were tired by the time the last group of well-wishers left, and we had missed supper.

"I've thought of that," Wang said. He pulled open a drawer of the table and offered me some cookies for our wedding supper.

Our first night together was traumatic. We got into bed and Wang turned off the light. I was scared. We didn't say a word to relax each other. We were both completely inexperienced and when all the fumbling was done, I lay shivering on my side of the bed in considerable pain. My body was screaming: "I don't want this again." The radiators, turned on for a couple of hours in the morning and again in the evening, had been off for hours. Cold and miserable, I started to cry, quietly so as not to wake Wang. So this was married life.

The next morning I went to the clinic. The doctor greeted me cheerily. "Look, who's here! It's our bride!" I blushed.

"What happened? You don't look well," the doctor said.

"I didn't sleep well last night." I couldn't bring myself to talk about anything related to sex. The embarrassment was excruciating, but I did need something to ease the physical pain.

"Um. I need help. It was very painful."

He laughed. "Comrade, you'll get used to it soon enough. What you both need is a little experience, that's all."

"But . . . I think I'm injured. Can't you give me something?"

"Well, take this," and he handed me a bottle. "It might help." I was too embarrassed to look at it in his office. Back home, I read the label: Vaseline. I told Wang I felt a burning pain and needed a week to heal. He respected my request.

Over the Chinese New Year holiday, soon after our wedding, we went to Tangshan to visit Wang's aunts. His mother had died of tuberculosis when he was a boy; his father lived in south China with his second wife. When his father made the move south, Wang's aunts had insisted on keeping him with them in the north; they weren't going to let their nephew be raised a southerner.

"My father's sisters were really unhappy when he married a southerner," Wang explained. "When one of my aunts says something critical about my father's wife, the other aunt says: 'Well what do you expect from a southerner?'"

As Wang was giving me this briefing on our way to Tangshan, he appeared to have forgotten that my parents were both from the south and my family's lifestyle was still basically southern. Our eating habits, for instance: southerners generally eat rice with every meal and, even though we lived in the north, that's how it always was in our house. My mother didn't like the things made from wheat flour that northerners sometimes substitute for rice: steamed bread, noodles, and dumplings called *jiaozi*.

Wang's aunts viewed southerners as being sly and crafty; as making good businessmen, perhaps, but lousy relatives. Many southerners, meanwhile, regard northerners as country bumpkins, crude, ill-mannered and uneducated. Southerners pride themselves on being refined and cultured. We had this conversation about north versus south squeezed together in the hard-seat section of a train packed solid with holiday travellers. Local merchants plugged the aisle with baskets of produce and live chickens. I had worn my silk brocade jacket and felt very out of place.

Wang's aunts' place in the suburbs of Tangshan was a nice country-style house kept warmly heated by a *kang*, a large brick platform that is the centre of a home in the northern countryside. A pipe running from a coal stove sends in hot air which collects underneath the kang. Families sleep side by side on the warm platform; they also sit cross-legged and eat on it.

The aunts had saved up rationed food so they could offer us meat and fish and egg dishes. It was a good meal, but I wasn't used to sitting cross-legged to eat and felt quite uncomfortable. I also wasn't used to sleeping on a kang. Wang's aunts had thoughtfully put extra padding underneath, but it still wasn't as soft as a bed and I tossed and turned for most of the night.

The next day we did a tour of Wang's other relatives. Everywhere we went I was asked the same three questions: "How old are you?" "How many brothers and sisters do you have?" "How much do you earn?" They were surprised to hear that a woman was earning seventy-eight yuan a month. I was proud to be making an above-average salary, but I felt uncomfortable about advertising the fact, because Wang was earning less. His fifty-six yuan a month was the basic salary for university graduates. The general view was that men should earn more than women. The only reason I was getting more was that I had had a head start. By the time Wang started working in 1957, I had already been working for six years and had had several pay rises. These were more frequent before the Great Leap Forward; once the campaign began in 1958, pay increases were almost non-existent. My 1956 salary of seventy-eight yuan, for instance, stayed the same for twenty-three years.

Back in Beijing, Wang and I had exactly two more weeks of normal married life before the first major disruption. The pattern established in our courtship continued: he waited on me hand and foot. Every morning I would wake to find warm water in a basin for me to wash my face. Having risen an hour earlier, Wang had even spread the toothpaste on my toothbrush.

One month after our wedding, I was sent to the countryside for a year to be ideologically "re-educated" through toiling alongside the hard-working peasants. Those selected for re-education had a non-proletarian family background and a perceived need for ideological reform. I was an obvious candidate.

The prospect of a year-long separation came as more of a blow to Wang than it did to me. My fear of sex had started to abate, but I still didn't mind the idea of some time alone. Wang did my packing for me, and dug out his old army clothes for me to wear when working in the fields. He looked downcast as he waved goodbye to me at the station.

About forty of us were setting off together for Xingtai county in southwest Hebei province. We were of various ages, from different work units; some were party members, some not. The six people from my work unit were all assigned to villages close to each other so we could meet on our days off for political study.

I was assigned to Dongjing'an village, population 300, along with the other woman in the group. Hui was a party member who was thought to need a little ideological fine-tuning. She and I were assigned to the same production team.

Except for very remote areas with low population, the whole of the Chinese countryside was now organized into production teams, production brigades and people's communes. Each village had several production teams; together these formed a production brigade. Several brigades, or villages, formed a commune,

Hui and I were given a small room in the village party secretary's home. We ate with the family, who had three young children, giving them some money and our small monthly ration of grain and cottonseed oil. Meat was not available unless pigs were slaughtered for special occasions, such as National Day on October 1. Each family then got its share according to the number of people in the household. The same method of distribution was followed when a cow, donkey or horse died. But we could see that the party secretary's family got more than its share: the butcher came after dark to bring them innards and lard.

A week after we arrived, our colleagues assigned to other villages came to ours for the first of many political study meetings. Hui chaired the session.

"First, I must make a self-criticism," she began. "I cried as we were leaving Beijing. My husband has been criticized for his right-deviationist thinking and I was worried about him." She lowered her head and her voice. "I let myself succumb to petit-bourgeois sentimentality. I should not have wept."

There was silence as people considered how to respond. I didn't say anything, but felt glad that I was stronger than Hui. After all, I hadn't cried when I left my new husband.

"As a party member, your emotions shouldn't be so fragile," one man said. "That's why we're here: to be tempered, to learn from the peasants their proletarian values and stalwartness."

Early the next morning I was wakened by a shrill male voice. "To work! To work!" I squinted at my watch. It was only half past five and still pitch black.

"The men of the village start working now," Hui explained. "The women start a little later because they have children to feed. But we're cadres, so we should go with the men."

Getting up to the production team leader's rallying cry would become routine over the months ahead. But wrenching myself out of bed in an unheated room on that first bitter February morning was difficult. I pulled on cold clothes as quickly as possible. I hadn't yet learned to keep them under my quilt at night. We broke the ice that had formed overnight in the porcelain washbasin, splashed water on our faces, brushed our teeth and raced out. We were the first to arrive. The team leader kept up his shouting while we shivered and squatted on our haunches, watching sleepy figures emerge from the shadows to join us. It took three-quarters of an hour for everyone to assemble.

"This morning," the team leader announced, "we're going to turn up the soil in the lotus pond. It's going to be hard work because the soil is half frozen." It really was hard work. The soil was muddy on top and frozen solid underneath. I dug in my shovel and was unable to pull it out.

"Don't dig too deep," said an old peasant man. "Here, use my shovel. It's sharper than yours." I was touched by this gesture.

Then the man looked around to make sure the team leader was out of earshot. "I don't know why you city people are here," he said. "And this isn't women's work. Look at your delicate hands. They're meant to hold pens, not shovels."

"We're here to learn from you, Grandpa," I explained.

"To learn from us?" He shook his head and resumed shovelling. He was faster with my dull shovel than I was with his sharp one. "What can you learn from us? How to get muddy hands and muddy feet?"

Sweat was rolling down Hui's forehead. She kept stopping to wipe mist off her glasses. Poor woman. She was in her forties, a bit plump and even clumsier than I was with a shovel.

We did all kinds of work in the fields, from sowing to harvesting. Most of the time men and women worked together, but there were some jobs the men tried to avoid. They didn't, for instance, like weeding in the millet fields because it had to be done with a short-handled hoe and men didn't like to bend or squat when they worked. Xingtai is in a major cotton-producing area. Men also didn't like picking cotton because the work wasn't "tough" enough. It was considered delicate, women's work and so only handicapped or old men worked alongside the women in the cotton field. In other words, to get men to do their share, the work had to be "just right" – not too hard and not too soft.

The most backbreaking work was wheat harvesting. First we had to learn how to use a sickle, then how to wield it rapidly and efficiently because everybody was expected to keep pace with the group. Working side by side, we had to move along our rows at the same speed, in the same direction, or else we might accidentally slash each other. We cut wheat for more than twelve hours at a stretch, from sunrise to sunset.

During the harvest, our lunch was sent to the fields and it was only then that we got a fairly solid meal: steamed buns and vegetable soup. The buns made from fresh wheat were really appetizing, but I was often too tired to enjoy them.

As 1959 wore on, the food shortages worsened. When winter closed in and the days grew shorter, we reduced our intake to two meals. The midday meal would be cornmeal gruel and a chunk of cornbread; the evening meal would be more gruel. Later, cornbread was replaced by yam-flour bread, which was purplish brown in colour, sticky when warm and rock-hard when cold. Sometimes elm leaves were mixed in with the dough to add bulk.

The team leader's wife worked in the canteen and was constantly inventing ways to stretch the ingredients. She enjoyed cheering us up with variations on our meagre diet.

"Come to my place tonight," she said to me one day. "I'm going to make you some noodles."

I couldn't believe it. "Where on earth did you get enough flour?"

"You'll see," she said with a smile and sauntered off.

The noodles she prepared didn't look different from ordinary noddles but they did taste different. And they were more slippery. But they tasted delicious to me. Eventually, she divulged her secret ingredient: the inner bark of an elm tree, ground to a powder and mixed in with corn flour.

Wang wrote to me three times a week. His letters read like a logbook, with everything he did from morning to night recorded in strict chronological order. He also wrote that he missed me. Instead of moving me, his words of longing left me cold. To me, some things, when expressed in Chinese, never sounded right. For example, I could say "I love you" in English, but not in Chinese. It was something we just never said.

My letters to him were much shorter and less frequent. After a day's work I was too tired to write anything by the flickering light of an oil lamp. Soon, the number of letters I was receiving became the subject of gossip in the village, and a matter raised at one of our political study sessions.

"Comrade Zhang, I really think you should tell your husband not to write to you so much," Hui said. "You know that kind of emotional attachment isn't healthy. And the time you spend reading and writing letters could be better spent on political study and integrating yourself with the peasants.

"Furthermore, how do you think it looks to the peasants when you receive a letter every other day? It looks very extravagant, because most of them will never receive a letter in their entire lives. It's as if you're saying to them: 'Although I'm stuck here temporarily in your backwater village, I'm still going to keep in touch with my more interesting life in the city.'"

I conveyed the gist of Hui's lecture to Wang and he reduced the flow of letters to no more than one a week.

Wang decided to visit me over the May Day holiday. The villagers, especially the women, were excited at the prospect of having a look at my husband the letter-writer. As it happened, Hui had to attend a meeting in another village over the holiday and so I would have our room to myself.

Throughout Wang's three-day stay, women and girls of all ages stood in the doorway to my room in twos and threes, staring and giggling. I left the door open during the day, because shutting it would be interpreted as shutting them out. And that certainly would have earned me another lecture.

I hadn't seen Wang for three months, but I hadn't really missed him. I felt uncomfortable with him in bed, as if nothing he did was right. He kept asking me what was wrong, but I didn't have an answer. I was angry with myself for feeling dissatisfied.

Even during his visit I couldn't take any extra time off, so I took him with me to the fields. During the breaks, as I stretched out on the grass to rest, the peasants teased Wang:

"Look how tired she is! How long did you keep her up last night?" said one.

"If I hadn't seen my wife for three months, I'd keep her up the whole night, too," said another.

Wang laughed, but I was embarrassed. Peasants joked all the time about sex and their bodies, and I felt uncomfortable hearing their rough humour.

Wang left after three days, looking sad.

Peasants did not get days off. If they wanted time to run personal errands, they had to ask for leave from the production team. The disincentive was that they didn't earn any work points for time off. Work points were calculated on the basis of quantity and quality of labour performed, and peasants in the communes were paid accordingly. Ten points were awarded for sowing, twelve for digging, 14 for rice transplanting, and so on. Women normally received fewer points than men for exactly the same work because, the team leader explained, "women are less productive."

Those of us sent to the countryside from the city had a slightly different set of rules. We worked six days in the fields and had one day off. But on the "day off" we were expected to assist the commune in other ways: help a peasant write a letter, or teach them to count. We also did this kind of work in the evenings after a day in the fields. I taught one group how to read and write. On our days off we also worked hard at "integrating with the peasants." We would visit them in their homes, ask them about their lives and answer their questions about ours. We had been instructed not to accept any food offered by a peasant, but this was an obvious point in a year when famine was stalking the land. If someone repeatedly pressed food on me, I took a tiny nibble, said how good it was and handed it back.

Once every two weeks we had another "day off" for political study sessions. We studied Chairman Mao's works and the latest documents from Beijing. Once a month we walked three hours to the county seat of Xingtai to have a wash in the public bath house.

Most of the villagers never went at all, but we city people looked forward to our monthly soak in the big communal tub.

While in town we also treated ourselves to a restaurant meal. I always ordered the vegetable dumplings and tried not to look too closely at the sausages in the display case. I knew they were made from hogs infected with trichinosis. Pork marketing was a state monopoly and so in theory bad meat should not have been in circulation. In reality, there was a lot of trichinosis in the pork supply and many peasants were falling sick because of it.

Every peasant family had to raise at least one pig to sell to the state. If state meat inspectors found evidence of trichinosis, they would not buy the animal. But fattening up a hog represented a huge investment for a peasant family and they rarely discarded diseased pork. Peasants believed cooking the bad meat under pressure, and longer than normal, would rid it of toxicity. They cooked it this way and then sold it locally.

You could see the larval worms that caused trichinosis in the raw pork displayed in markets: small white spots that when squeezed would discharge pus. It was even more dangerous when the meat was frozen, because then you could not see the tell-tale white spots. This diseased pork was much cheaper than other meat and peasants bought it because, at times, it was all there was.

Another reason disease was rampant was that the pigs raised by individual families were often fattened on human excrement. The hole in the Ren family's latrine, for instance, fed directly into an underground pig sty. I never got used to hearing a pig slurping around at close quarters below me as I squatted in the latrine. Looking down, I could see its snout.

The village tried starting a communal canteen and daycare, just like the cities had. But neither worked. People doing different kinds of work in the fields returned home at different hours, so there could be no set time for communal meals. And there was no place big enough to hold everyone. Daycare was supposed to free women to work in the fields. The village children were all looked after by two inexperienced young women, but when the mothers returned from work, they found their children with soiled pants and dirty, scratched faces. And the children missed the loving care they traditionally received from mothers or grandparents. Both projects were short-lived.

The village had a high infant mortality rate, as well as a high incidence of maternal death in childbirth. Midwives' equipment was not always well sterilized and infection was a frequent complication. With so many babies dying, parents took to giving their offspring ugly names. They believed that the more delicate the name, the more delicate the child's constitution would be; the nicer the name, the more likely it was the child would attract the attention of evil. Even the devil couldn't love a child named Stupid Dog or Little Stinky.

After ten months in the countryside, we were allowed back to Beijing in time to bring in the New Year of 1960. One man in our group, a young newlywed, had fled the village months earlier. "My wife misses me so much she's going crazy," he told me before he left. "I have to go." Soon after he returned to Beijing he was picked up and re-assigned to the countryside, this time for good.

We were all glad to be going home. There had been more and more grumbling in our group as time wore on, and over increasingly petty things: who was getting more attention from the peasants; who got a bit more food at one meal. I put it down to homesickness; trivial things loom large for unhappy people.

As the train pulled into Beijing station and I spotted Wang on the platform, the idea that I had a husband and that Wang was him seemed very strange. After almost a year apart, he, too, seemed uneasy. We sat silently on the long bus ride home.

Soon after, I learned I was pregnant, and that moment marked the end of our sex life together. We stopped touching completely. I didn't know what was wrong; I just knew I wasn't interested. We never talked about it. We were like two strangers, wrapped in separate quilts.

Chapter Seven

LITTLE SWALLOW

During my pregnancy, food became scarcer than ever. Immediately after the ruinous Great Leap Forward, several natural disasters in 1960 dealt their own severe blows to agriculture. The pressure of debt repayment to the Soviet Union after fraternal relations soured also put an unforeseen burden on the economy as a whole.

Fruit had become a luxury item in Beijing and I would have had none at all had I not had limited access to surplus stock from a dining-room for foreigners. Our import-export bureau ran it for the businessmen who visited for negotiations. If there was anything left over, it was sold off once a week, and we were allowed two kilos of whatever was available. Wang carefully managed our supply so that I had one piece of fruit every day.

We could see that by the time our baby was born, the situation would be even worse. So, like many other families, we began to raise chickens. I bought four chicks that we kept in a box lined with cotton-wool. But despite our efforts to protect them from the chilly April weather, only two of the chicks survived after the central heating was turned off, as always, on March 15.

The vendor had assured us the chicks would be egg-laying in no time. "You see? These are females all right!" he said, turning each chick around so I could examine its rear end.

"But how can you tell?"

"Don't worry, comrade, I've been doing this all my life. I assure you these chicks will grow up to be hens."

The man was either a huckster or having an off-day on the job because both our surviving chicks grew up to be roosters.

One evening in late October, I felt the baby coming. At government work units you could have the use of a car and driver in an emergency; Wang arranged for transportation and accompanied me to the hospital. The nurses advised him not to hang around because there was no knowing how long it would take.

Sometime after midnight I was wheeled into a big delivery room that already contained five moaning women. Two and a half hours later, our daughter was born. Luckily it was an easy birth; anaesthetic is still not used for childbirth in China, even if labour stretches for twenty-four hours or more.

When the woman doctor lifted the baby's legs to show me it was a girl, I couldn't stop giggling. The gesture reminded me of the chicken vendor as he tried to convince me my roosters were hens.

"It's hard to believe it's your first child," the doctor said. "You're lucky it was so fast." That it was such a good delivery did seem to be just luck. We were given no prenatal classes on breathing and pushing.

When Wang came back in the morning, his daughter was already several hours old. We looked on enviously as another new father walked by with a camera. How wonderful to be able to take a picture of your newborn.

Wang brought me my first meal after the birth, which my mother had prepared: millet porridge with brown sugar. "Your mother says the millet will warm your belly and brown sugar will get rid of the poison in your system," he said.

We named the baby Yan, which means swallow. She had big eyes and long eyelashes, and was adored by everyone in the family. Wang and I were both happy we had a daughter. I had always wanted one and Wang didn't really mind. He figured we could always try again for a boy in a few years.

During the five-day hospital stay, I tried to breast-feed, but there was never enough milk. The nurse was cross about this: "I don't know what those big breasts of yours are there for. They're all flab and no food for your baby."

Milk was strictly rationed. I was only able to get some by presenting a letter from the hospital certifying that I was having trouble nursing. Until she was a month old, Yan was entitled to one small bottle of milk a day, about half a pint. The ration was gradually increased as she got older, to a maximum of two pints. But as soon as she turned two, she was cut off. In the countryside there was no milk at all unless you kept a goat and didn't mind drinking its milk, unpasteurized.

Virtually all food was rationed in those days, even the common winter cabbage. Along with the baby's birth certificate, new mothers were given a coupon entitling them to extra rations. It was a one-time offer and you had to buy the food all at once.

My special ration after childbirth was a kilo of meat, four times the usual monthly ration; two chickens (normally chickens were available only on major holidays and then, only one chicken per household); and two dozen eggs. The usual ration per household, regardless of the number of people, was half a kilo, or about eight eggs a month. We also killed our two roosters to add nourishment to my diet. Wang made me cornmeal porridge every night before sleep to help me produce the small amount of milk that I was able to offer Yan.

I spent most of the standard fifty-six-day maternity leave at my parents' place where my mother helped with feeding the baby and washing the diapers. Wang came by after work and we all ate together, but it was hard when the only dish on the table containing any meat was reserved for me. My parents, both in their sixties, ate meal after meal of stewed cabbage.

"Don't do that, Zhimei," my mother would say when I picked out tiny pieces of meat from my dish to place in my parents' bowls. "There's not much meat, but if you eat it all, you and Little

Swallow will benefit. If each of us eats a small portion, it will do no one any good." Sharing rations became a problem in some households, and in some cases even caused families to split.

Many living quarters were like student dormitories; each family had one room and cooking was done in the corridor. Some people kept the pots chained to the stove; otherwise, hungry people wandered in and stole the food you were cooking, along with the pot. To buy a new one, you needed a ration coupon; to get a coupon, you had to wait your turn, which could take months. The coupons were more valuable than money.

Back at work after my maternity leave, we were frequently assembled to be told of a new item being added to the ration list. The party secretary would deliver a sober lecture about the difficult times and call on us all to pull together. When soap went on the list, we were given a day's notice.

"Rationing of soap starts tomorrow," the party secretary announced. "Stores are still open but I expect none of you to rush out and stock up. That would be unprincipled, because the country faces a serious shortage."

Although most of us heeded his warning, one man in his sixties panicked. He went into a store on his way home and bought several bars of soap. Another colleague saw him and reported the purchase. The next day, we were called to another meeting. The old man stood up, head bowed.

"Comrades, I made a selfish mistake," he said softly. "I must struggle harder in the future to overcome my outmoded ideas of individualism."

For those of us who had little in the way of savings, life had become very difficult. One of the government's responses to the supply-and-demand problem was to experiment with a two-tiered pricing system. Goods that were not generally available on the market could sometimes be found, but at five or six times the normal price.

"High-price restaurants" were opened. You took a number,

waited in line for several hours and then spent ten yuan on a meal that normally would have cost two. But at least the meal was available.

Apart from constant worries about food, life was quite peaceful, until Little Swallow was eight months old. In June 1961, government offices in Beijing began cutting staff in an effort to reduce the growing bureaucracy. After the "Three Difficult Years" of shortages and famine that followed the Great Leap Forward, the authorities decided the population of Beijing should be reduced to lessen the strain on the capital's resources. The Ministry of Foreign Trade cut its workforce by nearly forty per cent. The first to go were those from "inappropriate" families or with "complicated social connections."

My sister Wen, who worked in the same building as me, called on the office phone one day: "I must see you right away." Something was wrong. I dashed to meet her half way.

"I've been transferred to Anhui province," she said glumly. She had tears in her eyes. Everything was moving so fast. Only two weeks ago my closest friend, Feng, who had been my roommate in Berlin, was transferred to Xinjiang in the remote northwest. And now my sister to Anhui, a poor province in central China.

When my transfer came a week later, I was stunned. I thought I was among the trusted, that I had been sufficiently politically active and had demonstrated my loyalty to the party during political campaigns. Wang and I were both told we were needed in Harbin, capital of Heilongjiang, a province in the northeast bordering on the Soviet Union. The party's assignments were not open to negotiation. We packed our things, sold the few pieces of furniture we had and decided to leave Little Swallow with my mother until we knew more about the situation in Harbin.

On our last night in Beijing, my mother prepared a farewell dinner. I kept everyone waiting while I fulfilled a wish. Hua went with me to a new photographic studio where you could rent a Western wedding gown to have your portrait taken. My image of what a real bride should look like came from the Western films I had seen in the late 1940s. My sisters had had Western-style weddings before Liberation, whereas I had detested the political event that Wang and I had had for a wedding in our office canteen. The fancy old-style wedding was no longer socially acceptable, but I felt I had missed something and wanted to make it up to myself. Hua helped me put on makeup for the portrait, just me, alone, in a gleaming white gown.

Although I accepted a lot of the new thinking of Mao's China, I had also retained ideas from my formative years, which were lived, after all, before Liberation. In my adult life, it was a constant struggle to ignore these embedded notions. When, on occasion, my old self did emerge, it was usually then that I made a mistake, in society's eyes, and was criticized.

I was late for our farewell dinner, but happy. Later, as our train pulled out of the Beijing station, I could see my mother wiping her eyes with a shaky hand. Tears rolled down my cheeks, too. I didn't want to leave Beijing and all my relatives. I knew that once you were transferred out of the city it was very hard ever to get back. I had never been to Harbin, had no idea what it was like or what kind of work I would be doing there, where we would be living or when we could have our daughter with us again.

I was miserable but felt I had no right to show it. Following the party's orders was the obligatory duty of a league member. I believed it was not even right to think contrary thoughts, let alone complain or request special treatment.

We arrived in Harbin only to find we were not expected: there was no work for us and nowhere to stay. We lived for a month in a hostel before we were told that foreign languages were not needed, neither Wang's Japanese nor my English.

I became moody. I missed everyone in Beijing, especially my daughter. Nothing about Harbin seemed right — the way people dressed, their accent, the food. And you had to wait so long for seasons to begin and end; the weather was at least a month behind

Beijing's, and it was bitterly cold in winter.

We were both assigned to the provincial grain bureau. I worked in the research department, filing scientific studies all day. When we asked for a room to live in, we were told there was none vacant. "I hope you don't mind staying separately in the men's and women's dorms for a while," the head of personnel said. "It's a temporary difficulty you'll just have to accept."

I didn't want to live in a dormitory with complete strangers, and so I searched our work unit's buildings and eventually found a small room that was empty. It had no furniture or toilet, washing or cooking facilities. We moved in two single beds from the dormitory, found an old wardrobe abandoned on the playing field and stacked our suitcases to make a table. That part of the building was unheated, and we lived there until it was too cold to bear. Finally we were given a room in a residential building not far from the Songhua River.

Wang spent most of his time after work in the office. I was lonely, but had no energy to make new friends. We talked less and less; neither of us could be bothered to take the initiative. A gap between us widened that neither of us dared touch.

Finally one day, I got straight to the point: "I'm miserable. I hate everything here. And I find we have so little in common."

Wang was angry. "You're so difficult to please. I do everything for you and still you're unhappy. I do the cooking, I do the washing, I bring in the coal, I take out the ashes, I swat flies for you while you're napping. I make everything as comfortable as possible for you. What more do you want?"

"Did I ask you to knock yourself out for me? No! So don't try to make me feel guilty. Look," I said, softening my tone, "I just want to try to find out what's wrong between us."

"I can tell from the letters your friends in Beijing write you that you've complained bitterly to them about life here. Do you really think that's the way to handle difficulties? Why can't we work out these problems by ourselves?"

"How dare you read my letters! Don't I have the right to tell my friends how I feel?"

"I'm shocked at how you've changed since we came to Harbin," Wang said, avoiding my question. "Do you know what people are saying about you behind your back?"

"I don't care. You can't expect me to go around with an idiot grin on my face when I'm not happy."

"Well, if you're so miserable, file for divorce!" He stormed out, slamming the door behind him.

I flung his quilt and pillows out into the hallway and locked the door. He came back later and knocked at the door, but I wouldn't open it. So he went to Chen, an engineer who was the boss in my department, and asked for help.

Chen knocked gently. "Comrade Zhang, open up. Let's have a chat." I didn't respond.

"Don't act like a child. Open the door," he said.

Still no answer. "Now listen," he said, irritated now, "I'm asking you to open the door. You're not angry with me, are you? You could at least show me a little respect."

I unlocked the door. Wang was standing behind Chen, clutching the quilt and pillow.

"It's late. Let's not talk about anything tonight," Chen said. "But we'll have a chat tomorrow."

Wang and I said not a word that night. We slept in our two single beds as we had done ever since moving to Harbin. For more than two years, we had slept in the same room, but never touched. We never talked about it, and I didn't know how he felt. Maybe we were both scared to have another baby because life was so difficult now. Abstinence was the only birth control method we knew.

In the morning, I went to see Chen.

"That was not very impressive behaviour last night, Comrade Zhang," he said. "I was surprised by it, actually, coming from an educated person like yourself. Tell me what's wrong."

"I want a divorce."

"Wait a minute. Think carefully before you say that. This is a serious matter."

"I've given it a lot of thought already and I mean it. I want a divorce."

"But the two of you seem compatible. You're just being childish again. Look, comrade, take the day off and think about your situation. Think about what it would mean to be a divorced woman. And think about the humiliation you would cause Wang."

Wang was nervous when he heard what I had said to Chen. He hadn't expected me to have the courage to broach the idea of divorce. As a leading member of the youth league, he believed he should rely on the party even in personal matters. He reported everything to the personnel department.

Li, who worked in the department, came to our place one evening when I was alone.

"You have a nice home," he said. What he meant by that, I didn't know. Was he admiring the two cots, the rickety wardrobe or the table made from suitcases?

"I hear you're thinking of separating from Wang," he said. "Tell me about it. Are there any conflicts on basic principles?" By that, he meant political principles.

"We don't get along."

"What do you mean? You're both league members; you work for a common goal. He respects and cares for you. He's an upright and politically active person. Aren't these qualities enough, in your view, to make a good husband?"

It was starting to feel like an interrogation, and I was irritated. "Surely it's not for a third person to say whether a couple gets along? The fact is, we don't. We have no common interests. I feel no affection for him. We rarely talk."

The political preaching started in earnest. "As a league member, Comrade Zhang, you know full well that our personal interests should conform to the interests of the state and the people. There are proletarian interests and bourgeois interests. You should consider carefully which interests your behaviour conforms with before you make an irrevocable decision."

For a minute I didn't know what to say and just stared at him. There had been a time when I could discuss my personal life in political terms, but I couldn't do it now. There was too much at stake.

"Do you know that we are husband and wife in name only? I'm desperately lonely in this marriage. We rarely talk and we haven't slept together in the two years since I became pregnant."

My blunt words stunned him. "I can't really say anything about all that," he said, with obvious embarrassment, and left soon afterwards.

Divorce was rare in China in the early 1960s and, as in most other things, politics ruled. If your husband had turned against the state or the party, or been the target of a political campaign, divorce was seen as justified. Incompatibility was simply not an acceptable reason for wanting to separate. Emotions were considered abstract, bourgeois preoccupations. A woman who divorced for personal reasons may as well have worn a large scarlet letter around her neck – B, perhaps, for bourgeois; or I, for immoral. I lost track of the number of times I was told our marital problems were not real, that they were all in my head.

There were no divorced women at my workplace. I had no friends in Harbin, no allies, no one I could talk openly with, who would understand. It soon became public knowledge that I wanted a divorce, and suddenly everyone was distant. Many evenings, I strolled by the Songhua River, feeling lonely and isolated, and tormented by the question: was I doing the right thing?

I knew if I stayed in the marriage, Wang would be happy, I would regain the respect of my colleagues, and Yan would not have to face the stigma of having a divorced mother. But as hard as I tried, I could not silence the stubborn voice within that said if I stayed in the marriage, I would never be happy. I sensed there was more to life than this cold, uncommunicative marriage. To find out what more there might be, I decided I was willing to pay the price, to face the shame of being a divorced woman and shoulder the extra responsibilities of a single mother.

My talk of divorce offended the personnel department and I was transferred to work in the library of a training school run by the grain bureau. I liked the job better; working with books was more interesting than filing documents. And I had time to read. But the transfer was intended as a punishment, because the school was far from my home. I had to take a bus and then a tram, and the wait for both vehicles was often half an hour or more in the bitter cold. Because we never had enough to eat, I felt the chill in my bones. My clothes were no match for Harbin's winters.

I moved into the single women's dormitory, sharing a room with three others. I made it clear to Wang that whether or not he agreed to the divorce, I was not moving back in with him.

At Chinese New Year, in February 1962, I went to Beijing to see my daughter and to talk with my family. My nephew, Dong, brought Yan to the station to meet me. After eight months apart, she barely remembered me. I burst into tears when she reached out gingerly and said: "Ma."

I'm sorry, Little Swallow, I thought. You'll have to grow up without a father.

My mother was still in good shape, if a bit more bent. "Yan is a heavy baby to carry," she said. My father was still as withdrawn as ever.

I waited for Hua to come home for the weekend so we could talk over my problems; I longed for a shoulder to lean on. She had been assigned to teach at the technical school of the Capital Iron and Steel Works, far out in a suburban county. After supper on Saturday, I asked her to come and talk in the inside room.

"I'm having trouble with my marriage and I don't know how to handle it." I started to cry. Hua wasn't sure what advice to offer because she herself had been twice unhappily married and twice divorced.

Hua is a kind and gentle woman, the prettiest of us all, with a lively imagination and considerable artistic talent. She had always wanted to be a writer of children's books, but she never had the opportunity. She has had a hard life; she even had to give up one of her children because she couldn't afford the expense. Her second husband drifted into petty crime and was imprisoned soon after the birth of her fourth child. Our mother was worried that Hua would collapse under the strain of supporting so many children on a salary of forty-six yuan a month and she persuaded her to give the new baby away to a childless couple. It pained Hua to do so, but she also felt she had no choice. At first she visited the baby regularly, but the adoptive parents grew uneasy. They didn't want the child to know her natural mother, and Hua reluctantly agreed to stay away.

Now, as she struggled to give me the right advice, Hua's voice was as soft and humble as ever. "I really don't know what to say, Zhimei. I've long given up searching for love. Even if you gave me eight more chances I wouldn't be able to find the right man. I was very unhappy in my marriages. I want you to be happy, but I don't necessarily want you to follow my example. Think carefully before you do anything."

Without letting my parents know what was on my mind, I returned to Harbin after two weeks, ready to take the final step.

Wang knew my mind was made up and that there was no use trying to change it. "There are some things we need to talk about," he said, soon after I returned from Beijing.

"Like what?" I asked.

"Like childcare expenses and how we'll divide up our assets," he said. It sounded ridiculous to use the word "assets" to describe the radio we had bought for 150 yuan after our marriage. That was the only valuable we had.

"I've made a list of everything," Wang continued, handing me two sheets of paper. Four quilts, one blanket, four sheets, four pillows, two pots, a dustpan. He listed every little item we had in the household. I was furious.

"If all that junk means so much to you, keep the whole wretched lot. I only need a pair of sheets and a quilt.

"I want Yan to live with me," I continued, "and I won't ask you for any money." I was earning more than Wang and I thought paying child support would make it difficult for him to remarry. I didn't realize the financial burden I had taken on until I started to send half my salary to my mother for Yan's support. But as I had renounced any child support from Wang, I was allowed to keep our savings of 200 yuan, about three months' salary.

Because there were no disputes, the procedure for obtaining a divorce was as simple as for marriage. We went to the local civil administration office, sat in the corridor and waited our turn. I was nervous and tried to calm myself by humming the "Blue Danube" waltz. I knew life was not going to be easy after the divorce, but I saw no alternative. Wang assumed a nonchalant air. We were both acting.

We were called in. "What are your problems?" the clerk asked, peering at us over his spectacles.

"Ask her," Wang said.

"Incompatibility," I replied.

"Do you mean ideological incompatibility?"

"No," I said, "emotional."

"Emotional incompatibility? That sounds vague. What does it mean?"

"We don't get along and have both agreed to a divorce," I said, starting to worry that our request would be rejected.

"Is that true?" He turned to Wang, who sighed and nodded.

When the clerk learned I was not asking for any child support, he was surprised.

"Are you sure, comrade, that you know what you're doing? Do you realize you'll have no right to ask for any financial support from this man as soon as you sign this paper?"

"Yes, I do," I replied. He must have thought I was very stupid to accept such terms. We both signed the document and, with that, were divorced. We paid nothing. Divorce was free.

Wang fell ill soon afterwards, a relapse of tuberculosis he had contracted in the army. Using the youth league secretary as intermediary, he tried to convince me we should get back together, but I wasn't tempted. In later years I wondered whether we could in fact have worked things out if real marriage counselling had been available, and not just political lectures from our bosses. Within a year, Wang had remarried.

I was lonely after the divorce and felt I had no one to blame but myself. Why hadn't I been strong enough to call off the marriage when I first felt he was not the right man for me? I missed my daughter dreadfully. In those days, to comfort myself, I often hummed a lullaby called "Little Swallow" that I sang to her when she was a baby.

I didn't like my job and I longed for my friends back in Beijing, but I knew a return was impossible. Twice I tried to get a job in the capital; twice I was refused. When I applied back at my old work unit, the answer was: "Once you're out, you're out." When I tried at a different place, the answer was: "There's something about your 'social connections' that indicates you're unfit to work in Beijing."

Chapter Eight

I FELT THE HORROR AT ONCE

In the summer of 1964, I was transferred to the Harbin Foreign Languages Institute, happy to get the chance to become an English teacher. I taught English by day and in the evening read every book on teaching I could find.

I was twenty-nine, older than most of the two dozen new graduates assigned to work at the institute. Deng, a woman in her forties who was a dean of the English department, appointed me to be a senior teacher. My task was to help select those in the group who were qualified to be teachers; those who didn't make the grade would become teaching assistants. I had all contenders take a practical test and marked them on the basis of language skills and teaching ability. Some of the party's favourites were not very competent, and I didn't put their names forward to be teachers. This infuriated the school party committee: I had not put "politics in command" when making the selection.

At a meeting called to "debate" whether political credentials or professional competence were more important in a teacher, school president Fan said the former yardstick was proletarian, while the latter was bourgeois. And that was that. The debate was over and I had backed the losing side.

Things became pretty bleak after that. Fellow teachers reported evidence of my bourgeois tendencies to the party committee. One teacher told them I had said my only comfort in life was my daughter. I might as well have said: "There is no place in my heart for the party and the state." Yan was then four years old and living in Beijing with my parents. I saw her twice a year, at holidays, for an annual total of three or four weeks.

"I'm really miserable," I said to Lei, a woman colleague. "I have to talk to someone about all this."

"Why don't you speak to the new dean?" she suggested. Our department had been led by two deans; now they were adding a third. "He seems to be an understanding, intellectual type. Perhaps he'll be able to help."

That evening, she took me to meet Dean Jia in his room on the ground floor of our dormitory. He stayed there during the week and on weekends went home to his family, who lived downtown. He was a short man, with dark skin and an intelligent look.

Jia listened attentively as I poured out my story. The more I said, the more upset I became, and I started to cry.

"Cheer up. I understand how you feel," he said, handing me a clean cloth handkerchief. "I think president Fan is over-reacting. I'll talk with the leaders tomorrow and see what can be done."

I was grateful for his words; it had been a long time since I had heard a sympathetic remark.

"Do you feel better now?" he asked gently. I nodded and got up to leave. Then I remembered the handkerchief I still clutched in one hand. "I'm sorry, it's dirty. I'll wash it for you."

"No need for that. I can do it myself. Come and see me any time you feel like talking." At last! – a leader who was considerate and sincere.

I talked to Jia a few more times, taking comfort in his supportive attitude. Because he had taken my side in the conflict, he soon fell out with the school president. How could I have known that Jia would soon pounce, expecting payment for his solicitude?

It was a warm spring afternoon and most of the school was out on the field in front of our dormitory for a sports day. I wandered into the building to cool off and as I was walking upstairs to my room I bumped into Jia on the landing. "Odd," I thought. "He lives on the ground floor. Why was he upstairs?"

"Zhimei, I've been looking for you. Can you come to my room?" he said. "A button has come off my shirt. I wonder if you'd sew it on for me." Strange request from a man who could wash his own handkerchiefs, but he was, after all, a rare ally.

I finished the mending in a couple of minutes. "Is that it?" I asked, quickly rising to leave. I felt uneasy.

"Stay with me a little while," he said. "You attract me so much. You have a nice figure." He moved forward and grabbed my upper arms with two sweaty hands. "You speak beautiful English. I can't stand it any more."

"No!" I yelled, struggling. His grip was firm.

"Shhh, you don't want them to hear you outside, do you? That wouldn't do your reputation any good. I'll be good to you. I'll help you improve your situation." Where had I heard that line before, in just such a situation? But, unlike Berlin, this time I did not fight off the attack. Oh well, I thought. I don't have a friend in the world and here at least is some sort of comforter.

When I went back to Beijing for the summer holidays to see Yan, Jia wrote to say how much he missed me. He also asked me to come back two days early, and I returned on the day he suggested. As I stepped off the train, I was startled to see him waiting on the platform. Why had he taken such a risk to meet me openly? He was a married man. If our relationship became public knowledge, we would share the disgrace. The words "immoral person" would go into both our files. Even years later, we could be denied job promotions because of it.

"Don't go back to school," he whispered as he bustled me out of the station. "I want to take you to the summer resort for cadres."

"But that's no place for me!" I said. "People there know you. How will they view me?"

"Don't refuse me. Please! Nobody will suspect anything. I'll book you into a separate room. I'll say you're my cousin."

I knew we would be taking a big risk. But, against my instincts, I agreed to go: he was my superior, and I was cowed. We took a bus, transferred to a ferry and crossed the Songhua River to the Sun Island resort. It was a nice place, only five minutes' walk from the bank of the river. Bungalows were arranged around a courtyard, and Jia saw to it that I was given the room beside his.

I felt uncomfortable about the way people were looking at me. Was it because I was wearing a white sleeveless top, rather skimpy attire for the times? Or was it because we both wore a guilty look? I fought with my conscience and decided to leave. Jia begged me not to, but this time I was determined. When we got to the ferry dock, the last boat of the day had just departed. I had no choice but to stay.

To avoid meeting cadres from the school, we ate in a little restaurant instead of in the resort's canteen. After supper we went for a walk along the river. I was edgy, sensing that we were being watched. When we sat by the river, a motorcyclist stopped a few metres away and tinkered with his bike until we left.

When we got back to the resort, four men were playing cards in the gatekeeper's room. "That's odd. They've never been there before," Jia whispered as he walked me to the door of my room. "I'll come to visit as soon as they leave." But the game continued late into the night. Perhaps the card-players had instructions to stay at their post until morning.

The second day was even less romantic than the first. I was convinced we were being trailed wherever we went. Two days of that was enough and I went back to school, making sure a train from Beijing would be arriving at about the same time so no one would suspect I was coming from anywhere different. As I was walking into the dormitory with my suitcase, I ran into Rong, a deputy dean in my department.

"So you're back from Beijing. When did you arrive?" he asked.

"Ah . . . this morning." My face was burning.

"Only this morning?"

I sensed something had gone wrong. I smiled weakly and dashed upstairs. The next morning I was summoned to the office of the party committee, to face three scowling officials.

"Where were you the day before yesterday?" the woman in charge began.

"I . . . ah . . . got back from Beijing yesterday," I stumbled.

"Damn," I thought, "why can't I lie? I always give myself away."

"You're not being honest. We know everything. Do you really think you can do something like this without anyone noticing? Do you know what will happen if you don't tell the truth?" Then she reminded me of the party's policy of "showing leniency to those who confess their crimes and severity to those who refuse."

I kept silent, and she kept pushing. I was determined not to say anything because I knew they would be questioning Jia at the same time; any inconsistency in our stories would put us both in an even more difficult position.

"You won't be teaching this week," the woman cadre said. "You will stay in your room to write your confession. Don't take any chances. And don't imagine that we can't punish you further."

I knew I was in big trouble. A woman teacher was assigned to me for the week, to make sure I didn't talk to Jia, or try to commit suicide. But that same afternoon I bumped into him in the hallway. By chance, we had both been allowed out of our holding pens at the same time to go to the toilet.

"I've told everything," he hissed. "Tell the truth."

And so I did.

"It's clever of you to acknowledge you had a sexual relationship with Jia," the party interrogator said after reading my first effort. "But surely you're aware that that's not enough. You must detail exactly how it began and when, where and how many times you had sex with him. The more detailed it is, the more sincere you'll show yourself to be."

As I wrote it all down, my sense of humiliation deepened with each new detail I provided. The confession undoubtedly would go into my file and remain there for the rest of my life.

I don't know how the school authorities explained my week's absence to the other teachers, but many of them treated me like a stranger when I returned to work. Now I was under even more pressure than I had been when I first took my problems to Jia.

Strangely, the school president, Fan, started to become quite friendly. He invited me to his home for dinner and his wife, once very hostile, became almost pleasant. Fan had several talks with me and each time we met I would criticize myself further for my mistakes. His response was always: "You need to raise your political consciousness and take the party's interests into greater consideration."

"Have I not told them enough?" I wondered. "What more can I do?" I soon found out.

One day I was summoned to see Rong, the deputy dean. "You really shouldn't let Jia get away with it this easily," he said.

"What do you mean?"

"You've been insulted and disgraced. You could go to court, you know, and lay charges."

I was startled. "Charge him? With what?"

He paused for a moment.

"Rape."

I was stunned. Finally, I understood: I was being used as a pawn in a power struggle between Fan and Jia. My relationship with Jia was to have been Fan's trump card.

I refused to comply and, as a result, Fan threw me to the wolves. The school authorities had promised to keep it all secret, but my private humiliation soon became public politics. My confession was circulated among the teachers and students. Later, a team from provincial party headquarters was called in to investigate the matter, to stir it all up again.

My misbehaviour, however, was soon overshadowed, drowned out by the opening shots of what was to become the Great

Proletarian Cultural Revolution. Power in the country, we were told, had been usurped by intransigent capitalist-roaders, who were still lurking from top to bottom in society. None of the political campaigns that had already convulsed the country had been able to root them out, and mobilizing the masses to expose the crimes of these class enemies was the only solution.

Classes were cancelled and wouldn't resume for six years. "Suspend classes and make revolution!" was the slogan of the day. All our time was devoted to studying Mao's works, writing big character posters, attending criticism sessions and milling about in mass rallies. Walls around the campus soon were covered with thick coats of paper. In a cycle that was to go on for years, new posters went up every day, only to be pulled down the next.

At least two groups made a fortune out of the Cultural Revolution: the Ministry of Forestry's paper mills and the garbage collectors who stripped the posters off the wall at night only to find layers of new ones there the next day. The Cultural Revolution provided the latter group with an inexhaustible source of income, for they could sell the old poster paper for recycling. They seemed to me to be the only people who were doing something mildly constructive as millions of others were busy tearing the country to pieces.

Several revolutionary groups formed on campus, but none wanted me. I was flattered when one group asked me to sign a petition simply because they needed more names. But most of the time I felt painfully isolated.

At about this time, my parents' home in Beijing was ransacked. The same thing was happening to millions of other families around the country as the Cultural Revolution's youthful shock troops, the Red Guards, swung into action. A contingent of teenagers from a nearby school for girls, wearing army uniforms, red armbands, and pigtails, marched into my parents' courtyard. A young neighbour offered them the information they sought; she pointed her finger at my parents' place, and her own family was spared.

The Red Guards pulled everything out from the chest of drawers, the wardrobe and suitcases. The pile of clothes that grew on the floor included the expensive silk gowns and coats that had been bought for me, by the state, before I was sent to Berlin. But mostly the heap contained the well-worn clothes of my nieces and nephews. My sister Hua could barely support her three children on her own, so new clothes were rare.

"Who are you trying to fool, keeping patched old clothes around to try to hide your wealth and expensive tastes?" one of the Red Guards shouted. "Do you really think you can get away with such an obvious trick?"

Another girl, tossing things out of a cupboard, seized on my father's photograph album and began scrutinizing each yellowed picture. The earliest ones recorded his years in Japan: one showed him on an outing with Japanese classmates; in another, he was dining with Japanese colleagues and geisha girls; and tucked casually in among the others was the well-thumbed picture of the mystery woman, whom my father refused to identify for us. This kimono-clad beauty was just: "I don't remember – some woman." Later pictures showed my parents posing stiffly in studio portraits taken on their anniversary. My father had been proud of showing us the album when we were young, but after he lost his job he pushed it to the back of a cupboard to gather dust.

"Why are you keeping these pictures?" The girl swung around to address my father, who was standing, slumped, in the doorway.

"They're just old photos, nothing special. I'd actually forgotten they were there," he answered softly.

"Don't think that we don't know what's going on in your head!" the girl shouted. "It's obvious you're dreaming of a comeback of the 'good old days' when imperialist troops controlled China! Why else would you have kept photographs of Japanese devils so carefully all these years?"

My father could only look on sadly as she ripped the kimono-clad beauty out of the album and tore her to pieces. Another Red Guard had started a bonfire of books out in the courtyard and the album was soon hurled on to the pyre.

My fifteen-year-old nephew Dong had his photograph album torn from his hands: "Burn this one, too!" I had bought the album for him in Berlin and in it he had kept every picture of himself ever taken.

"Out-and-out bourgeois!" The Red Guard spat at Dong's feet. "Look how many pictures you've had taken of yourself! What extravagance!" Dong, who was shy by nature, sat biting his lip, on the verge of tears. He had treasured those pictures and his eyes never left the album as it went up in flames.

"Where are your valuables, your jewelry?" one girl, busy slitting open a mattress, demanded of my mother.

"As you can see, we have nothing valuable," my mother said.

"And we can also see the fine clothes you wore in those pictures," the girl retorted, motioning toward the bonfire. "We know the lengths you rich people will go to, to conceal your wealth."

One girl placed a chair on the table, climbed up and yanked open a trap-door in the ceiling. She stood on tiptoes, searching the space under the roof with a flashlight. But she found nothing. "These people are cunning," she said in frustration. "They've obviously got themselves a really good hiding place."

"Remove these!" The girl who had burned the albums, who seemed to be the group's commander, was pointing to the stone slabs on the steps outside the front door. Her troops set to work, digging and prying out the heavy stones, one by one. All that lay underneath was good yellow soil.

The girls were disappointed and didn't want to leave without some accomplishment to report. So they locked up the good clothes from my Berlin days and my mother's old mahjong set, made from ivory, in the wardrobe.

"These things don't belong to you any more," the leader said. "You bought them with money you acquired by exploiting other people. They will be confiscated. Beware of the consequences if you attempt to unseal this wardrobe."

Two months later, the wardrobe was taken away. Soon afterwards, my mother told me she had seen someone wearing clothes that looked a lot like mine.

"You have bad eyesight, Ma. Don't ever repeat what you've just said," I warned her. But I was sure she was right.

The Red Guards also took all our savings. The 200 yuan that Wang had given me in lieu of child support was gone. My parents lost their life savings of 100 yuan; Dong had to part with the 10 yuan he had saved from his pocket money.

On the day after the ransacking, my mother went to the kindergarten at the usual time to pick up Yan, who was then five years old. The teacher used to be warm and friendly, but not today.

"Don't bring her back," she said.

"Why not?"

"Your house has been ransacked, hasn't it? We don't take children from bad families."

My mother gathered up the paper cuttings Yan had made that day and walked silently home with her, hand-in-hand. Poor girl, she was thinking, what crime have you committed? You can already quote reams of Chairman Mao and the only songs you know are political. I've heard you sing while you're playing: "The core force leading our cause is the Chinese Communist Party/The theoretical foundation guiding our ideas is Marxism-Leninism."

It was not unusual for people, frightened of being found with anything old or valuable or foreign, to do the work of the Red Guards for them. My sister Wen burned all the pre-Liberation stamps from her husband's valuable collection, which had included some rare Qing dynasty stamps. She also burned all the foreign stamps, sparing only Chinese stamps issued since Liberation.

An old friend of my mother's who received money regularly from her daughter in the United States panicked when she heard Red Guards banging at the door. She hastily flushed U.S.$1,500 down the toilet. Another friend clambered on to his roof in the middle of the night and threw a bag containing his wife's jewelry as far as he could. "I don't care who picked it up," he told us later. "But whoever it was, were they lucky or unlucky to find it?"

My parents were forced to sweep the streets. Every morning before dawn, their group of seven "monsters and demons," as they were called, would assemble at the neighbourhood committee office. The committee, run mostly by older women with little education but impeccable political credentials, is the main apparatus of control at the neighbourhood level in Chinese cities. "Ask forgiveness from Chairman Mao!" a neighbourhood committee biddy would bark. The monsters and demons, all in their sixties and seventies, were made to bow to Mao's portrait, repeating: "I'm guilty, I'm guilty. I beg Chairman Mao's pardon."

They were given brooms, which were too big and heavy for some of them, including my father, who was already quite frail. Back and forth he swung the unwieldy broom, for hours every day. His grandchildren knew he was back when they heard him trying to bang the dust off his clothes and shoes before entering the house. He swept the street for years, without a single complaint.

I never did hear my father make a disparaging remark about the communist government. And he always applauded the engineering achievements, such as the building of the bridge over the Yangtze River at Nanjing, or the extension of the railroad out to Urumqi in the far northwest, saying: "This would not have happened under the old regime."

Things became much worse for me after my colleagues learned what had befallen my parents in Beijing. I was labelled one of the "bastards" of the Five Black Categories: landlords, rich peasants, counter-revolutionaries, bad elements, and rightists. Later, four more categories were added to the list: traitors, revisionists, capitalist-roaders, and intellectuals. The latter was the dumping ground for teachers, also known as the "stinking ninth category."

More posters went up: "Dragons bear dragons, phoenixes bear phoenixes; the offspring of mice can only dig holes"; "If the father is a hero, the son is a brave man; if the father is a reactionary, the son is a bastard." Before speaking at meetings, people had to declare their family background, for example: "My father is a landlord and I am a bastard."

People from proletarian family backgrounds belonged to the Five Red Categories: workers, poor and lower-middle peasants, soldiers, revolutionary martyrs, and revolutionary cadres.

It takes time to get used to reading posters that hold oneself up to stinging public ridicule. I was deeply embarrassed when, after the first ones went up detailing my crimes, a student called out as I scurried by the posters: "She has no shame! She even has the nerve to show up." But later I could manage a silent sneer at some of the more ludicrous charges against me:

"She corrupts her students' minds by telling them stories from Western literature. She advocates a Western lifestyle, teaching words like knife and fork, butter and jam."

"She keeps powdered milk and cookies on her shelf, and eats them before going to bed. Some young teachers innocently follow her bourgeois example."

"She does not put politics first. Once, when she was teaching the word 'favourite', she pointed to her jacket and said: 'This is my favourite jacket.' Why didn't she hold up Chairman Mao's quotations and say: 'This is my favourite book'?"

"She likes bright students and doesn't show enough concern for students from good family backgrounds. This shows her lack of class feeling."

"She wears bright clothes; sometimes she wears her jacket unbuttoned. She leads an indecent life."

I was soon ordered to move from the sunny side of the building over to the shady side. Sunny rooms were henceforth reserved for revolutionary teachers.

One cold winter's night, we were startled from sleep by a banging of gongs at around 2:00 a.m. "Everybody out!" a man was shouting.

When I poked my head into the corridor, Fu, a fellow teacher, was being dragged from her room. Other teachers were putting a dunce cap on her and forcing her to hold a gong. They made her march up and down the icy corridor for an hour, repeating: "I am guilty. I beg Chairman Mao's pardon." After each repetition, she had to strike the gong, a sound I had hated ever since I had first heard Peking Opera. We were all forced to stand and shiver in our doorways and watch her humiliation. It seems that Fu, an arrogant young woman who belonged to one of the "revolutionary" groups of teachers, had fallen foul of an opposing group. The factional warfare had begun.

"This is what will happen to any of you if you ever try to resist," shouted the head of the faction that had the upper hand.

"Down with Fu!" someone in the captive audience yelled out, eager to show his loyalty.

New methods of torturing people began to appear. And new directives from Chairman Mao kept pouring in. Whenever a new one was issued, no matter what time of day or night, we would have to leave our dormitories and parade in the streets in celebration. Lanterns and banners prepared for the occasion would be waiting for us to pick up at the school gate. Even if it was forty below zero, with a howling wind, we would still march. "We have a fervent heart, loyal to the party! We are not afraid of the cold!" one earnest marcher shouted as our faces began to freeze.

"Resolutely support Chairman Mao's newest directive!" we bellowed, holding the lanterns up and waving the banners. "Long live our great teacher, great leader, great supreme commander, great helmsman Chairman Mao!" It was imperative to address Mao using all of the four greats, and to get them in the right order.

The procession from the school to a main road and back took at least an hour and a half. Our cheeks were frozen, our hands numb; we lost feeling in our feet because we were walking so slowly. But no one dared complain.

In the next phase, intellectuals with ideological problems like myself were assigned to do manual labour to remold our attitudes. This process of rebirth was called "casting off one's old self." My job was to clean the corridors and toilets in the students' dormitories. For a while I did it with Dean Deng. She, too, had been accused of being a bourgeois intellectual. We usually worked in silence, afraid of being overheard making a complaint or an offhand remark about the students. She would start mopping the corridor from one end and I from the other and we would meet in the middle.

As for the toilets, the scene was the same every day: a mountain of faeces in each bowl. The smell was indescribable. The toilets, the squatting kind, were often blocked and always left unflushed. Sometimes we would have to push so hard with the plunger that we would be spattered with the bowl's filthy contents. Toilet duty must have been harder for Deng than for me; she was always fastidiously clean herself.

"You know what it is," she once grumbled as we mucked out neighbouring cubicles. "Many of the students are from the countryside and they've never seen a flush toilet before. They have no idea how to use it."

"Be careful!" I hissed. "Don't say such things." If anyone had overheard her, we would have been accused of slandering the children of poor and lower-middle peasants.

Because light bulbs were rationed, new bulbs disappeared fast. In the end, the school stopped replacing dead or missing bulbs altogether. And so the boys' toilet presented us with an additional problem. When it was dark, the boys just stood at the washroom door and urinated. Every morning a pool of urine would need to be mopped into the toilet.

Although no classes were being taught, because of the system of guaranteed jobs we were still being paid. Revolutionary students and teachers could come and go freely from the school, but people like me had to ask permission to leave. I was worried about how Yan was faring in Beijing, and at one point I asked for, and was granted, a month off.

I was concerned about what might happen to my things in my

absence, so I went through them carefully before I left, ripping up many of my pictures and letters. My roommate, a revolutionary teacher, did her best to avoid me, a target of criticism. But that evening, as I was sorting through my things, she kept popping into the room, first to pick up a handkerchief, then a book, later a pair of knitting needles.

It didn't occur to me at the time that she was reporting my every move to Red Guard students. When I returned from my trip, only my bedroll was still where I had left it. The students had taken everything else away, all my clothes and pictures and the few items of value I still owned: a Parker pen, a German alarm clock, some ivory chopsticks, a couple of state bonds.

"We were planning an exhibit to show how bourgeois you are," explained Hao, a student leader. But the exhibit never materialized because they realized my belongings were hardly enough to prove a bourgeois lifestyle.

Trains were unbelievably crowded that winter. Every day, tens of thousands of students, teachers and factory workers poured into Beijing to be reviewed by Mao in Tiananmen Square. This was called "establishing revolutionary ties," and the revolutionary rebels, as they called themselves, travelled free of charge. Few had ever had the chance to travel before, let alone to the capital. Free travel, plus an extended paid vacation, was like winning a lottery, and some toured half the country. To board a train, all they needed was a letter from their local revolutionary committee. I bought a ticket, though, because people like me could not afford to take chances. On the trains you either had to show a ticket, or your revolutionary credentials.

It was a twenty-three-hour trip to Beijing. The seats were all taken when I boarded, and the aisle was packed. There was nowhere even to put my bag down to sit on. My head started to throb from the thick tobacco smoke. I shifted from one leg to another, trying to ease a growing pain in my back. I had been standing for about four hours when I noticed an old peasant man crawl under a seat, where he curled up and heaved a sigh of relief. "I couldn't possibly do that," I thought. Another hour passed, and another. Then I thought: "Can't you change some of your 'stinking ninth category' habits and be more practical?" So I, too, crawled under a seat and curled up.

Having the weight off my feet was like heaven, though not a particularly pleasant one. My face was pressed up against a pair of dirty cotton shoes. Many people on the seat had taken off their shoes and the smell was awful. Decaying fruit peels, watermelon seeds, sunflower seeds, egg shells and bits of discarded food had formed a sticky mass on the floor of the train. The smell of urine coming from the toilet, which had long since run out of water, was nauseating. I was hungry and thirsty, but also exhausted, and soon fell asleep. When I reached Beijing, hours late, I was itchy all over; my mother suggested I had picked up fleas on the train, and she was right.

The overloaded trains were often hours behind schedule. Before the Cultural Revolution, the railway had a reputation for good, punctual service. Now its rigid timetables were called evidence of "bourgeois control." It was revolutionary to declare: "I'd rather have socialist delay than capitalist punctuality."

I wanted to try to protect Yan, now six, from witnessing more of the violence and humiliation she had seen at her grandparents'. I decided to take her to stay with my sister Wen in Hefei, capital of Anhui province. Wen and her husband had not yet become targets of the Cultural Revolution, and it seemed like a relatively secure place for Yan to be. In reality, there was no safe haven anywhere. It was just a matter of time.

Another consideration was that Wen had no children of her own and was happy at the prospect of Yan's company. Even in normal times Chinese children often live with members of their extended family when it seems the best arrangement. This sense of collective responsibility for children becomes especially important in times of upheaval.

Until then, Wen and I had both been sending a portion of our monthly salary to our parents. Money from their children was all they had to live on; there still is no universal pension system in China. Because Wen would now be supporting Yan, I took over contributing her share of our parents' upkeep.

My mother, who had taken care of Yan since she was eight months old, was crestfallen at my decision. Caring for her granddaughter had become the focus of her life. She stayed awake on their last night together, holding Yan, who slept beside her. My mother had become more bent in recent years; Yan was too heavy for her to carry, but she still liked to cuddle her. As the world went mad all around her, her granddaughter had been a great source of solace. It was heartbreaking to separate them, but I felt strongly that Yan would be safer out of Beijing.

The Yongdingmen train station was quite a distance from my parents' home, so Yan and I set off two hours in advance. We couldn't squeeze on to a bus, because of the steady flow of people into the capital. In those days young people could often be seen hanging from a bus, caught in a half-closed door as the packed vehicle lurched forward.

We walked fifteen minutes to a taxi stand, where we saw four drivers waiting for their next fare. Hearing us come in, the woman in the dispatcher's office didn't bother to look around. She had her back to us as she warmed her hands over a coal stove.

"What do you want?"

"A taxi to the Yongdingmen railway station, please."

"What's your family background?"

"Intellectual," I said. I could have lied, but she might have asked to see our residents' permits.

"No cars available," she said brusquely.

"But we're in a hurry. We'll miss our train," I pleaded.

"Forget it. Chairman Mao teaches us to serve the people. We only serve the people here — workers, peasants and soldiers."

As we left the taxi stand, I was close to tears. If we missed the train, I wouldn't be able to afford new tickets. Just then a pedicab rounded the corner, and the driver was sympathetic. During the hour-long trip, he pedalled as fast as he could. "Don't worry," he wheezed. "We'll make it. I'm old, but experienced." He got us there, just in time.

Yan, who had been used to being a bit spoiled by her grandmother, had to adjust to a new routine in Hefei. Wen and her husband both worked, so Yan was sent to a boarding kindergarten during the week. On her first day and night at the school, she wept bitterly. Wen had stuffed Yan's bag with treats, but that didn't seem to help. The change was too sudden for her. I stayed in Hefei for a few weeks until I felt she was starting to get settled. I wanted to stay longer, but I couldn't risk getting back late to Harbin and having another crime added to the list.

I knew it would be a shock for Yan when it sunk in that I, too, was gone. As the train moved away from Hefei, I felt as if my heart was being torn in two. Not much of my family was left intact, and now I had to leave Little Swallow again, without knowing when we might be reunited. In my mind's eye I kept seeing her tearful face as she asked: why had she had to leave Grandma, and when would I come back to get her. But I had no answers for her.

Soon after my return to Harbin I grew closer to Pang, another English teacher at the school. He was four years younger and one inch shorter than me. Now and again we would go out for a meal. More than once, Pang hinted that perhaps there could be more between us, but I thought we weren't compatible in that way.

Our backgrounds were very different. His father had died when Pang was eight. When his mother remarried she left Pang to be raised by his grandfather, an alcoholic old soldier who had had little schooling. Pang grew up in the poorest part of Shenyang, a rough area full of petty criminals. Having had to cope so much by himself at an early age, he was independent and resourceful. He was also open, energetic and caring.

But I thought that, like Wang, he lacked the refined upbringing of my own family. Before Liberation, my sort of background would have been considered "good breeding"; after Liberation, I suddenly came from a "bad family." I had tried hard to adjust to the new standards; I had married Wang, one of the new breed of revolutionary men who had fine ideals rather than refined manners. But somewhere in the back of my head I was still longing for the sort of man I had been raised to expect I would marry. And, having consumed a steady diet of Western films and novels in my youth, I also secretly hoped to be swept off my feet by romantic love.

Pang was no Rhett Butler, but I did like him a lot. He had a strong sense of fair play, and a seemingly endless supply of sympathy for the underdog. I was impressed by the way he took care of a classmate who had an abortion after her boyfriend dumped her. Others shunned her, but Pang's instinct was to go to her aid.

The accusations against me, that until then had been confined to wall posters, now spilled over into mass criticism sessions. I was nervous at the meetings; once I even fainted. I felt wounded as my students raised their fists and shouted slogans against me. They were the same students with whom I had spent long hours, taking pains to correct their every mispronunciation. But they all had their own reasons to join in. For my favourite students, who tended to be the most attentive in class, it was a chance to dissociate themselves from me and avoid being accused of currying favour with a bourgeois teacher. For the ones who were not hard working and had received poor marks, it was an opportunity to get their own back.

I was led away from one such session by Lu, one of my students. As a young boy he had been scalded in the face as the result of a kitchen accident. Skin grafts had helped, but there were still deep purple scars on his neck and face. Lu led me to a storeroom where the school's reference materials were kept. He worked in the library and this storeroom also functioned as his bedroom. "Sit!" he commanded. I sat, not knowing what to expect.

"Here, drink this." He handed me a mug of water. "Do you know what your crimes are?"

"I'm not sure." I was also not sure what was on his mind.

"Do you accept that you are an immoral woman?"

"I've made mistakes, but I'm not immoral," I said.

"Get up!" he said, moving toward me. His purple welts seemed an even more violent colour at close quarters. "Do you know that I can help you?" I stared at him in stunned disbelief. Then he grabbed me, pressed himself against me and started to kiss me.

"Let me go!" I shouted, struggling to escape. I couldn't believe my own student was doing this to me when I was in such a vulnerable state. I wrenched myself free and headed for the door.

"Stop!" he yelled. "Don't tell a soul about this. Even if you do, you know nobody will believe you."

Later I told Pang, who was furious. I begged him not to mention it to anybody. I was in enough trouble already.

Pang had become the only person I trusted on campus, and we saw more and more of each other. This caused gossip, especially because of our "unequal" political status. He was a member of one of the revolutionary groups and I, one of their targets.

One day I was summoned to appear at the headquarters of the Red Terror Group, radical students notorious for their violence. I was worried.

A few months earlier, Mao had authorized the Red Guards to lead the attack on the "four olds": old customs, old habits, old culture, and old thinking. But the situation was already spinning out of his control. Young people who had never before had any power, even over their own lives, suddenly found themselves wielding enormous amounts of it. Their lives were circumscribed and deeply frustrating, and they needed little encouragement to hit back at the authority figures close at hand – their parents and teachers. (Mao himself, revered as leader of the revolution, was beyond reproach.)

But most of these youthful activists didn't know how to handle power, and its abuses were already widespread. They had seen arbitrary arrest, illegal detention, torture and forced confession all done in the name of revolution. The communists had continued the Chinese tradition of rule by men, not by laws.

"What is law?" I had once heard a member of the Red Terror Group say. "I am the law."

I dreaded my 8:00 p.m. appointment with them.

"I'll go with you," Pang said. "I'm on fairly good terms with those students."

We arrived punctually at the classroom the group had declared its headquarters. I felt the horror at once. The room was kept dimly lit with red bulbs that had the characters Red Terror Group inked on them. "It is right to rebel," said a slogan splashed on the wall above Mao's portrait. Apart from two wooden desks and a few chairs, the room was bare. In the gloom, I could make out half a dozen figures.

A man with an army coat slung over his shoulders sat at one of the desks, puffing at a cigarette. I recognized him as a second-year student who was, in a previous incarnation anyway, very shy. A tall, broad-shouldered student standing beside the desk was well known for his powerful fists.

"We're going to interrogate her," the student in the army coat said to Pang, "and you keep quiet." He sent Pang to sit in a room across the hall, from where he had a clear view of the proceedings. The student then turned to me: "Do you know what your crimes are?" I stammered something about having kept in touch with Frau Hentze, who I had worked with in East Berlin.

"Isn't there something else? What about your private life?"

I hesitated, not sure what he wanted. I thought perhaps an all-purpose confession would satisfy them. "I've committed serious mistakes," I said.

"You're an immoral woman, a fox spirit!" he screamed. "How many men have you had? Tell us everything! You've corrupted party cadres, and now you've got your hands on one of the revolutionary teachers. Do you really think you can get away with this?"

"Kneel! Kneel in front of Chairman Mao!" yelled the student with the famous fists. "This is what you deserve," he said, yanking off his belt. A slap of the belt stung my face and my glasses flew off. Someone snatched my hands away whenever they flew up to cover my face. I don't know how long the whipping and punching lasted; I don't know how many people took part. I was only aware of the pain, the grunts of my attackers and my own cries for them to stop.

Suddenly, they did stop. I fumbled about on the floor, groping for my glasses. Someone shouted to Pang: "Take her home!"

On the way home I asked Pang why the beating had ended so abruptly. He said he had taken one of my attackers aside and asked if the group was aware that Lu had tried to sexually assault me while carrying out a little freelance interrogation of his own. "You're calling her immoral? Do you know what one of your own did the other day?"

They were startled by Pang's intervention, and it stopped the beating. Had I brought up Lu's behaviour, no one would have believed me. But coming from Pang, a revolutionary teacher, they had to listen. The next day, after interrogating Lu, they expelled him from the group for "misbehaviour." It seemed incredible to me that they were going through the motions of following any kind of behavioral code at all at this point. But for them, expelling their comrade was a way of showing that they still had discipline. Of course for them, beating me black and blue was also a fine display of revolutionary discipline.

Pang took me back to my room. I could barely walk. When I appeared at the door, my roommate was so frightened that she looked away from me. "What did they do to you?" she whispered. I was too feeble to reply. "Do you want to look at yourself in the mirror?" That was the last thing I wanted to do. I wanted only to lie down and try to sip some water. My head ached, my face ached, every part of me ached. My roommate ran to the clinic to fetch the doctor but he wouldn't come because, he said, he only treated revolutionary patients.

The next morning, I did look in the mirror. My face was swollen to twice its size and covered in bruises.

Pang went to the clinic and found a woman doctor with a reckless streak: "I don't care who she is. If she needs treatment, I'll go." When she examined me, she couldn't believe how badly I'd been beaten.

Not long after this nightmare, I married Pang, in late 1968. I was grateful for all he had done for me, but I did not marry him because I felt I owed him something. I could see that he was a good person, with a strong backbone. But we were both aware that I was not madly in love with him and we discussed this openly.

It is traditional in China to take the long-term view of things, to plan carefully for the future and for one's children. But during the Cultural Revolution, when no one could predict what would happen next, we lived one day at a time. In that context, I had neither the time nor inclination to think long and hard about whether Pang and I were really suited to spend our lives together. With the country in turmoil, personal happiness was a secondary consideration. Trying to avoid political trouble, just staying alive, was our main concern.

When I was under attack, when the walls of the campus were plastered with posters criticizing me, when other people started to keep their distance, Pang stood firm. No matter what pressure he was under to do otherwise, he never said anything unkind about me, either openly or behind my back. In times of trouble he seemed to me like a strongman, holding back with muscular arms concrete walls that were caving in. I loved him for this.

Chapter Nine

DOWN WITH THE INTERNATIONAL
WOMAN HOOLIGAN!

In the summer of 1968, the target of the Cultural Revolution shifted from capitalist-roaders to intellectuals, the "stinking ninth category." Every day a new poster went up on campus summoning a "bourgeois" teacher to appear at a specified time at the Dictatorship Group headquarters, the core of the school's revolutionary committee.

Not surprisingly, my turn soon came. On the notice summoning me, my name was shown in boldface, but not upside down, as had been the case with "capitalist-roaders." I was terrified when the poster went up, but knew it was pointless to resist. If you didn't appear, they fetched you. The slightest defiance landed you in even more trouble. Once you showed up, you became the "object of dictatorship," as it was called. You were locked up in a classroom and interrogated for months.

It was the summer of 1968, and Pang and I had been married only three months. He went with me to the Dictatorship Group headquarters, carrying my bedroll across campus as students we passed along the way shouted insults. Hao, one of my former students and now one of my jailers, dismissed Pang, went through my things and confiscated a small pair of scissors. He told me to unpack my things, that he would be back in a minute or two to lock me in the tiny, darkened room that was now my cell.

I spread the bedroll out, stuffed my clothes into a pillowcase and placed my two metal washbasins – one for my face, the other for feet – under the bed. No books were allowed except the works of Mao. While I was wondering what to do next, another student appeared at the door, out of breath. It was Huang, who school party officials considered a troublemaker because he liked to ask questions in class and sometimes even to joke.

"I wanted to see you before you were locked up," he said.

I was shocked that he had come, and struggled to keep from crying. The slightest show of sympathy or kindness in those days would move me to tears.

"You must go at once," I said. "You'll only get yourself in trouble. The guard will be back any minute."

"I don't care," he said. "I have to tell you that I didn't want to attend the criticism session the other day. I want you to know that when the others pointed their fingers at you, I just sat and watched."

"I understand. I know you had no choice."

I remembered the session he was referring to. Classes had already been suspended, but I walked into my old classroom and found the floor papered with big character posters. Some of the students started to roll them up hastily when they saw me. I knew they were preparing for a criticism meeting against me; I didn't want to embarrass them, so I left quickly.

At the meeting called later that day, my students' criticisms stung me, but I didn't find the proceedings all that unbearable. It was mostly a shower of empty slogans, and I knew many of them had been forced to attend as a test of loyalty.

Four other people at the school had been detained before me: President Fan, labelled a capitalist-roader because he had demoted incompetent staff members who came from "good" worker or peasant families; Lian, a man in his sixties who had worked as a translator for the old regime; Ding, a man in his forties who had gone to university in London and had once worked for a foreign embassy in Beijing; and Guan, a cook who had worked in the police force during the Japanese occupation. I was the only woman in the group, and my crime had not been specified.

The canteen was about a block from the building we were being held in. That evening, we were led there by the student on duty who wore a red armband marked "Dictatorship Group." There were catcalls from all sides during our trip.

"Look, Ma, come and look. There's a woman in the black gang!" I turned at the sound of a child's voice and saw a small boy making faces at me. Poor lad, I thought, you shouldn't be part of this. If you've been told that what is happening is fair, what will *you* be like in ten or twenty years? In fact, the Cultural Revolution did produce a whole generation of ill-educated, selfish and undisciplined people who had no faith in anything. They were the "lost" youth, a decade or two older than the students who filled Tiananmen Square in 1989.

"Don't look around! Lower your head!" the guard barked.

Our gang of five was always taken to the canteen after everyone else had eaten and all the good food was gone. Before and after meals we lined up in front of Mao's portrait and asked for forgiveness. After the meal, we were marched back to our rooms and the doors locked again from the outside.

The first two weeks of detention were devoted to writing a confession. For days, I sat staring at the blank sheets of paper I had been given, uncertain how to begin. I started working for the new China in 1951 before I had even turned sixteen. Politically, I had always tried to follow the right line. Professionally, I had been hardworking and competent.

The only thing I could think of that could be construed as improper behaviour was my friendship with Frau Hentze, my East German friend. We wrote to each other until 1963, that is, for a couple of years after China's rift with the Soviet bloc. But I had always been careful about what I wrote in letters, knowing they were censored. Still, I was suspected of being a spy.

I laboured over my confession: "When Frau Hentze returned to Germany after a visit to China in 1955, we started to correspond. She wrote that she had married and that her husband worked for East German Customs. When she became pregnant, she wrote that she was afraid she would have a difficult childbirth because she was in her late thirties. So she tried to become as fit as possible by walking up and down flights of stairs many times a day.

"We sent each other presents on birthdays and at Christmas. I told her about my own marriage, and later about how it deteriorated. I wrote to her that I had custody of our daughter after the divorce. She wrote back, surprised that I hadn't asked for any child support. After that, she sent me things for Yan quite often."

That was all I could remember from our exchange of letters. I submitted my first confession.

The Dictatorship Group was irritated. I had not been specific enough, and they hauled me in for interrogation.

"Name every item she sent you," I was told. "Did you ever ask her for anything? Did you ever remark on the difficult life in China?"

And so, I handed in a list.

"Frau Hentze sent me the following items:
one pair of fancy nylon underwear (pink) after my wedding,
four pairs of nylons,
one pair of shoes (white),
baby clothes when Yan was born,
more children's clothes after my divorce,
four packages of powdered milk, (when I told her that some things were rationed in China).

P.S.: I should not have told her there was rationing in China. And I should not have told her that I had to pay import duty on everything she sent me."

The Dictatorship Group was not pleased with this second confession either. "Why did she send you things? Do people usually give things for nothing?" My interrogator then howled "No!" and went on to quote Mao: "There is absolutely no such thing in the world as love or hatred without reason or cause."

"Now tell me, why did she care for you so much?"

I shrugged. "We were friends. She liked me. I liked her."

"Stop trying to peddle your stinking bourgeois sentiments. Beware the consequences if you continue to be so stubborn," he warned.

A few days later, I was marched back to the interrogation room, which this time held four men I didn't recognize, wearing Mao jackets buttoned severely to the neck.

"Lower your head!" shouted one of the student-guards as I entered the room.

"Take your hands out of your pockets. Go to the middle of the room," ordered another.

"Apologize to Chairman Mao!" yelled a third.

I stood to attention in front of Mao's portrait, then bowed three times, repeating: "I apologize to you, Chairman Mao."

The interrogation commenced. It soon became apparent that the strangers were municipal-level security police, present because I had been implicated in another case.

I knew a librarian at another Harbin college, a bright, scholarly man who spoke six languages, including Esperanto. As president of the Harbin branch of the Esperanto Association, Xia had established contact with pen-pals all over the world who could write in Esperanto. These correspondents were said to be his network of spies and the language they used, which few in Harbin could understand, was said to be a code. On top of that, he had been born in Taiwan, where he still had relatives. He was arrested as a spy.

Like all of us, he was told to write down the names of everyone he knew in the city. I was on his list. This caused great excitement and his case was instantly linked with mine. What kudos if they could unearth a big spy ring!

"Was there anything suspicious in the things Xia talked about with you?"

"No."

"Did he ever talk about defecting?"

"No."

"Then what did you talk about when you met?"

"He was after me."

"Be serious!" the interrogator snapped.

The cross-examination lasted for several hours, going over and over the same ground. I just couldn't give them the evidence they sought to prove the existence of an espionage network.

That evening I was taken to a classroom for a criticism meeting, to be interrogated by fellow teachers. Pang, however, was not allowed to attend. The teachers all had their copy of Mao's little red book of quotations on the desk in front of them. I was told to stand in the middle of the semi-circle, facing my accusers. I made my usual bows and apologies to Mao's portrait. Then the bombardment began:

"What is your relationship with Xia?"

"Who else is in your group?"

"What are your means of communication?"

"What's your mission?"

"Why did your German friend send you things? What information did you give her?"

"What did you say against the socialist system in your letters?"

The questions were ridiculous, and I kept silent.

"Stubborn, eh?" yelled Su, a heavyset teacher. "You think you can get away with this? This is class struggle. Revolution is not a dinner party, neither is it painting or embroidering . . . Revolution is violence . . . " He was quoting a passage from Mao that all of us could recite. As he spoke, he unfastened his wide leather army belt. I knew what was coming and closed my eyes. After that, the only sounds in the room were the thrashing of his belt and his sadistic threats: "I want to see how tightly closed your mouth really is!"

I knew that resistance would only prolong the beating. I said nothing; no whimpering, no tears. I just braced myself to withstand the blows as best I could without reacting. After my earlier beating, at the hands of the Red Terror Group, my capacity for fear was greatly reduced. My attitude was: what could they do to me that was worse than that?

I don't know how long this assault lasted. During beatings, I lost all concept of time. After a while, a man went to whisper something in Su's ear. I learned later that he was being told not to leave any marks on my body. He put his belt back on. A few minutes later I was led out of the room, to shouts of "Down with the spy Zhang Zhimei! Down with monsters and demons!"

Pang was not supposed to know about the meeting, or the beating, but he found out and insisted on seeing me the next day. Normally, family members were only allowed to drop off basic necessities like soap, toothpaste and toilet paper, as well as a monthly food allowance. Talking to the prisoner was not allowed during visits. But this time, Pang brushed past the guard and marched straight into my room.

Silently, I pulled up a corner of my shirt to show him the marks on my body. "Bastards!" he whispered. "I'll make sure nobody dares touch you again." Before the guard arrived to pull him out of the room, Pang wrapped his hands around mine. Scared and lonely, I longed to feel his strong arms around me.

He told me later that he went straight to the school's People's Liberation Army representative to protest. He argued that the beating violated Mao's directive to "practise verbal struggle; do not resort to violence." This did stop further beatings, although the physical punishment would soon take other forms: "keeping company," for instance, in which the victim is forced to stand during round-the-clock interrogations until, limbs swollen, mind and body exhausted, they are ready to confess to anything.

Zhu, a former friend of Pang's, stole an old address book of mine from our home and handed it in to my jailers. By "keeping company" with me, they tried to get me to admit that the names in the book were spies in my network. Although exhausted after being on my feet throughout an all-night interrogation, I was able to resist confessing to this ludicrous charge. In fact, the lists of names and numbers in my old address book were not a code of some kind, as they believed, but the scores of ping-pong matches I had jotted down while organizer of an office tournament in the 1950s.

My dare-devil husband soon found a way to visit me again, at the Moon Festival, a holiday in early autumn that is normally set aside for family reunions. We were taken to the canteen for dinner a bit earlier than usual because our guards wanted to go home to their own families for the celebration. When I returned to my room, which was left open while we were away, I immediately smelled fruit. My washbasin was covered with newspaper, underneath which was a small mountain of pears and peaches.

"Shhh, Zhimei," a voice whispered. "I'm here, under the bed." It was Pang! My heart began to race. I lay down and whispered into the narrow gap between bed and wall: "How could you do this? It's so risky! You must leave at once!"

A finger reached up and stroked my cheek. "No, I'm staying here tonight. I've been watching for this opportunity. The guards are distracted today because of the holiday, and I'm sure no one saw me come in."

"You mustn't stay! Anything could happen if they found out. Please go. Please!" A tear rolled down my cheek and he brushed it away with his finger. There was silence from under the bed.

"Oh, Pang, I know you miss me. But not now, not here . . . . "

I was happy just to hear his voice, but terrified of the consequences if he was discovered. I went to the door, made sure no one was there and shoved him out of the room. After closing the door behind him, I collapsed on the bed in tears. Some family reunion!

The Dictatorship Group decided to let us out of our cells to do manual labour. I was glad; it had been two months since I had had much fresh air or exercise. The guard shouted, "Up! Up!" at 5:30 every morning as he unlocked the door. I carried my metal wash-basin, the one for my feet had to double as chamberpot at night, to empty it in the washroom. Then our gang of five lined up and followed the guard outside.

Once outside, the guard stood face-to-face with each of us in turn and bellowed: "Who are you?" We had to attach our "criminal title" to our name: "Fan, capitalist roader!" the school president replied. Every time I had to say mine, I cursed Lin, the inventor of my nasty label: "Zhang Zhimei, international woman hooligan!"

On our way to the canteen we had to shout: "Down with monsters and demons!" "Down with capitalist roaders!" After a while, the guard thought up something different.

"From now on," he said, "you'll denounce yourself." Now, as he marched us to the canteen, I had to shout: "Down with the international woman hooligan Zhang Zhimei!"

Every morning, we were put through our paces reciting three of Mao's works: "Serve the People," "In Memory of Norman Bethune," and "The Foolish Old Man Who Removed the Mountains."

"You, Lian, recite 'In Memory of Norman Bethune,'" the guard bellowed.

"Comrade Norman Bethune," Lian began, "a member of the Communist Party of Canada, was around fifty when he was sent by the Communist Parties of Canada and the United States to China . . . ." He recited the essay fluently, without a single mistake. The guard looked pleased.

"Now you, Guan, recite 'Serve the People.'" The school cook was semi-literate and had a terrible time trying to read and memorize Mao's essays.

"Um . . . our Communist Party . . . and, uh, New Fourth Armies . . . and Eighth Route Army . . ."

"Wrong order!" yelled the guard.

"No problem. I'll start again. Our Communist Party . . . uh . . . and the Eighth Route and New Fourth Armies led by our party

. . . " It was painful to listen to Guan's stammering, because we knew that sooner or later the guard would belt him.

"All men must die . . . uh . . . but death can vary in its significance . . . . To die for the people is weightier than . . . um . . . Mount Tang, no, no, I mean, Mount Tai . . . uh . . . but to work for . . . um . . . the capitalists . . . "

Slap! The guard struck him on the face. "How dare you distort the works of Chairman Mao! It goes 'to work for the fascists' and you know it. You'll pay for this stubbornness!"

Poor Guan! Distort this sacred text was the last thing he wanted to do.

The person ordered to recite "The Foolish Old Man Who Removed the Mountains" was the unluckiest because the piece was the longest of the three. My ability to memorize, trained from learning English vocabulary lists, helped me out.

During daily political study sessions we discussed these or other of Mao's works or selected articles from People's Daily. Then we worked the whole morning and afternoon, with a break for lunch, followed by an hour's rest. We only got the after-lunch nap because if they kept us on our feet, our guards would have had to sacrifice their nap, too.

The work was hard. We shovelled coal in the hot boiler-room or snow in the cold outdoors; we unloaded truckloads of bricks, sand and coal. For a while we worked in the kitchen, until someone complained: "How can we let class enemies prepare our food? Suppose they try to poison us?"

The school had three huge cellars where vegetables were stored for the winter months. Working in the vegetable cellar was my favourite chore, because I had some time to myself. I could hum a tune and sneak the occasional bite out of a turnip or carrot, or nibble on a stray cabbage leaf. The cabbages had to be turned over at least twice a week to stop them rotting, and each time they were shifted they shed some of their outer leaves. When spring came, often only the hearts were left.

Unloading coal was the worst job, because we had no place to wash ourselves thoroughly. For ten months, I didn't have a bath. Every weekend on our day off I used my two metal washbasins to give myself a good scrub: first I washed my hair, then my body, using one basin for the top of me, the other for the bottom half. If there was any hot water left, I washed my clothes. I did manage to keep myself reasonably clean.

But some of the men found it difficult. Ding's constant scratching caught my eye one day during political study.

"Something wrong?" I whispered.

When the political instructor looked away, Ding scribbled in English on the back of his notebook: "I've got these bugs all over my body. And they're spreading."

Even before Ding started scratching in political study sessions, he always used to clatter his teeth. He bounced his jaw up and down, and ground his teeth back and forth. He particularly liked doing this after meals; he said it was good mouth exercise and excellent for the digestion. Ding had brought some weird ideas back with him after his years in London, and we just assumed this was one of them.

But on the day Ding started scratching, too, our political instructor got fed up with his teeth-clattering: "What the hell is going on over there? Why do you move your jaw all the time? I'm going to take you to the hospital this afternoon and have them take a good look at your teeth."

Our jailers were getting bored with us; we offered them no new material in our endless confessions. They seemed as weary of detaining us as we were of being detained. In their frustrated state, some wild notions started to enter their heads. This particular guard became convinced that Ding had a sophisticated radio device implanted in his teeth and that when he was clattering his teeth, he was transmitting coded messages.

The guards had learned from my neighbours that, before my detention, I often used to type late into the night. I was preparing class notes, but that was too banal an explanation for them. So they carefully examined my 1930 portable Remington, suspecting each piece of being spy equipment.

About six months into my detention, things took a dramatic change for the worse when a hard-line faction called the Workers' Propaganda Team gained the upper hand in running the school:

"They're criminals, and you let them sleep on beds?"

"You feed them the same food as you eat?"

"They're still getting paid?"

The faction demanded change. Our bed frames were removed, leaving us only the straw pallets. Some people developed kidney trouble because they were sleeping so close to a cold cement floor. I escaped this added difficulty because the artful Pang managed to slip past the guard one day and leave me a thick feather quilt to put on top of the thin mattress.

Although we were detainees, we continued to receive our salaries because we were still considered employees. Jobs were assigned by the state and you were hired for life. Unless you committed a serious crime and were put behind bars, you could not be fired. Of my monthly salary of seventy-eight yuan, I was given eighteen yuan to pay for food and Pang was given the rest. He saved half for me and sent the other half to my mother in Beijing.

We were no longer allowed any choice in the canteen. The kitchen used us as a way of disposing of their leftovers, some of which had already gone bad. But we were allowed to buy as much rice and as many boiled yams as we wanted. I bought extra yams and kept them in my room to nibble on. Malnutrition caused some people's teeth to fall out. I was only thirty-three, but my hair turned grey. Poor nutrition was to blame; extreme stress didn't help.

The Workers' Propaganda Team was not very impressed with our school. Eventually, the number of people in detention rose to more than forty, about one-third of the staff.

"At this school, the majority of the staff are bad elements," the propaganda team leader declared. He obviously was not aware of

Mao's saying that "95 percent of our people are good."

The number of detainees increased as the scope of the persecution expanded; it was no longer limited to people who had a bad branch somewhere in their family tree or "complicated" social connections. Now, those who had "followed the wrong line" at the beginning of the Cultural Revolution also became victims. In some cases, old scores were being settled.

The teachers being punished were forbidden to communicate with each other, but most of us were happy to obey this rule since by now we had learned that talking was risky: words could be distorted or misinterpreted. Overhearing our guards gossiping about their charges was our main source of information. It seems that one man, a party member and department head, lost his dignity completely the instant the Dictatorship Group summoned him. "I'm guilty! I'm guilty!" he cried as he strode to their office. With each impassioned admission of guilt, he slapped himself on one cheek and then the other. His self-flagellation only won him the guards' disgust.

"Stop that, will you!" one of them yelled. "What a spineless creature you are! You've made the party lose face!"

An English teacher was detained because his five-year-old son had been overheard saying in kindergarten that disgraced former head of state Liu Shaoqi was a good man. He was accused of having taught his son to say this.

A teacher of politics was picked up because of a note he had scribbled in a book about the young Mao. The text said Mao was a voracious reader. He had written in the margin: "And so am I!" He was punished for daring to compare himself to the great helmsman.

Another teacher was detained because her father had fled to Taiwan just before Liberation. She fainted when the notice went up for her to report to the Dictatorship Group headquarters. She was eight months pregnant at the time. (With no classes to prepare, teachers had a lot more time on their hands in this period, and one result was that many families doubled in size. China's population soared.)

When I was first detained, I thought: "Why me?" But I looked around and saw that my fellow victims were not just the people of my parents' generation, who had been the regular and, perhaps, inevitable targets of previous political campaigns. With the Cultural Revolution, the scope of attack had broadened, and my own generation was now also under the gun. The brutality, it seemed, was to be repeated from generation to generation. With this realization, I accepted my fate as inescapable, and my attitude shifted to: "Why not me?"

For some of the time, I had a roommate. The first was a party member who worked in the school's personnel department. Her pallet squeezed next to mine took up all that was left of the floor space. She was an unpleasant woman who didn't share any of the common feeling and mutual sympathy that had developed among the other detainees.

Even in detention, she lost none of her arrogance. "Our problems are of a completely different nature," she said on her first day with me. "My mistakes fall into the category of contradictions among the people, while yours are contradictions between the enemy and the people."

Ying, my second roommate, was the victim of mistaken identity. She was accused of having belonged to the Kuomintang youth league. They interrogated her again and again, but in vain. She wouldn't confess, because it simply wasn't true. She would come back to the cell to write more self-criticisms, humming quietly to herself. She was cheerful by nature and the more nonchalance she showed, the more vengeful her interrogators became. This went on for months.

Later, it emerged that the testimony the school had received concerning someone by the name of Ying referred to a man. Even the leader of the Workers' Propaganda Team was angry about the mistake, and he yelled at our guards: "Can't you people even tell the difference between a man and a woman?"

Eventually, new directives were issued from on high and the detainees began to be released. Given that I had been among the first five to be detained, I kept expecting my release at any moment. It was worrying when I realized only a handful of detainees were left. Were we to be sent to labour camps?

One day as I was sweeping the stairway, Pang passed by and threw a tiny crumpled ball of paper at my feet. I left it there until I was sure no one was looking, then tucked it into one of my socks. Later I locked myself in a toilet cubicle and read the note: "Is there anything else you haven't confessed? They have nothing to prove you're a spy. Now they're thinking of labelling you a 'bad element' because of your personal relationships." I read the note a second time before flushing it down the toilet.

What else was there to confess? For days, I racked my brain. I had told them absolutely everything . . . except for one brief romance with someone soon after my first divorce. Could that be what they were after?

It was. The man in question, who was also under detention, had mentioned me in his confession. But they wanted admissions from both of us to seal the case.

I was desperate to get out of detention and so I, too, confessed. As a result, my poor husband had to face yet more malicious gossip. Luckily, our teachers were not so vulgar as to parade me through the streets with a string of worn shoes tied around my neck, as I had seen done to other women accused of having had sex outside marriage.

One day, I was led from my cell to the room that used to be the teachers' office. All the school's teachers were present. I was told to stand outside the room and wait until they were ready for me. It was a long wait. For once there was no one guarding me and at one point I slipped into the toilet.

There I saw my friend Zhen. For ten months I had not been allowed to talk to anyone, apart from fellow inmates, on equal terms. And now I was paranoid. Our eyes met and I shook my head, warning her not to speak to me. She opened the door of each cubicle to make sure no one else was there.

"They're planning to free you today," she whispered. "But be careful about your attitude in front of them. It will count for a lot." We stood, speechless, looking into each other's eyes. Zhen brushed a tear from her cheek, and left quickly.

A few minutes later, I was led into the meeting room to shouts of "Down with Zhang Zhimei!"

Two long rows of desks lined the walls, and every seat was occupied. I noticed Pang, his eyes cast down, reading or pretending to read something on the desk in front of him. I was told to sit behind the desk that faced Mao's portrait. Before taking my seat, I made the usual three bows and apologies to Mao. No one had told me to; by then it was a conditioned reflex.

I was invited to make a self-criticism. I said I was an immoral woman, who had led good male comrades astray. And I had damaged our national reputation when I accepted gifts from an East German woman. The head of the revolutionary teachers stood up and elaborated on these themes. He ended the litany of charges against me by saying: "From now on, you should study Chairman Mao's works more carefully and remold your bourgeois outlook.

"Those who agree she should be freed, hands up," he said. Everyone raised a hand, except Pang, who pretended to be scribbling in a notebook. It was his way of protesting both my detention and this final spectacle.

I stood up and thanked Mao, the party and the revolutionary teachers for releasing me. This conformed with the accepted view that everything they did was just. One slogan went: "It is just to release you; it is equally just to arrest you." I was led out of the room to shouts of "Down with bourgeois intellectuals!"

A few days later, a formal announcement was made at a mass meeting of the school's revolutionary committee: the spying charge against me had been withdrawn. But nothing was said about my wrongful detention. Admitting mistakes was not revolutionary behaviour. And certainly the good guys never had to admit mistakes in front of bad guys.

The case against me may have been dropped, but there were still signs that the "evidence" remained in my file. About a year after my release, the team of oil workers my brother belonged to was transferred to a new oilfield. But he alone was not allowed to go. He went to the personnel department to ask why. Normally, he would not have been told the truth, but the man in charge happened to be a former classmate. He told my brother that his file said that his sister was a spy.

My brother immediately cabled me: was this true? I was furious with him for not being able to work that out for himself. But I also felt sorry for him, because I knew this black mark would stay in his file for the rest of his life.

Pang carried my bedroll back home in the same way he had carried it from home ten months earlier. Home seemed much the same, except that the neighbours had become even more cold and uncommunicative. I was glad about this; people were going to leave me alone and perhaps that way I could avoid getting caught up in factional battles.

On my first evening of liberty, Pang took me out for a meal. At the restaurant, I heard him asking if I wanted to do the ordering. I was in a daze and couldn't answer. I just stared at the people around us, as if they were all just objects, as numb as I was feeling. The greasy plastic table-cloth, the loud conversations of beer-swilling men, the smoked-filled room, the food-smeared floor – I took it all in, but everything seemed so unreal, as if I were watching a movie.

Fish and pork dishes were placed before me. Seeing what state I was in, Pang had ordered for us. I picked at the meat dish, but put down my chopsticks without tasting the food. I felt as if I had lost all senses, including the sense of taste.

"Let's go," I said. "I think I need time to recover from oblivion."

Chapter Ten

STRANGERS AND PEASANTS

During my detention, the personality cult had deepened. Now nothing was available in bookstores except Mao's works; the only choice was whether you wanted the paperback or deluxe hardback edition. A set of Mao's works or a handful of Mao badges were now the only presents anyone exchanged. You got them as wedding gifts; you gave them as birthday presents.

Grown men and women collected Mao badges with the enthusiasm of eight-year-old stamp collectors. The badges appeared in different shapes and sizes, showing the great leader from different angles: profile, bust, full-length, sitting, standing; Mao as a young man holding an umbrella; Mao during the Long March; an older Mao in army uniform waving to Red Guards in Tiananmen Square. The badges were sometimes porcelain or plastic, but mostly aluminum. They were as small as a button or as big as a plate. Nearly every home had a sizable collection, pinned on red cloth and framed.

"If the Russians invaded and we had to run for our lives, I'd leave everything behind but my box of Mao badges. They would save me." This was one of Pang's favourite jokes; Mao was supposed to be omnipotent.

So much aluminum was poured into making enough badges to satisfy an 800-million-strong market that even Mao himself became annoyed. "Give me back my airplanes," he said. After that, we were told to hand in our badges for recycling.

The "loyalty dance" was another activity that had sprung up during my detention; a song and dance routine to express one's allegiance to Mao. The most popular song accompanying the dance was "The Red Sun in Our Hearts": "Beloved Chairman Mao, you are the red sun in our hearts/We have so many things to confide in you/We have so many passionate songs to sing to you/ Thousands of red hearts are facing the red sun."

Kindergarten children danced, old women with bound feet danced, the whole country danced. We raised both arms and swayed back and forth, tapping our feet at the same time. A latecomer to the dance, I somehow never got it right. I could waltz, tango and do the jitterbug, but I always looked clumsy doing the loyalty dance.

Every morning and evening, in a ritual more rigid than anything I had experienced at Catholic girls' school, we talked directly to Mao. It was called "morning requests for instructions and evening reports." We stood in a row in front of his portrait, bowed, recited some of his quotations, then asked him what we should do that day. We sang a rousing chorus of "The East is Red" and ended up with three repetitions of: "Long live Chairman Mao!"

After Lin Biao was designated Mao's successor, we began shouting an additional slogan. Wishing "long life" was reserved for Mao alone, as it had once been for the emperor. The slogan about Lin went: "Eternal health to vice-chairman Lin!" But that was struck from our repertoire with Lin's sudden downfall and death in a suspicious air crash in 1971.

After all this hearty shouting, a group leader gave out orders, as if they emanated from the Chairman himself. In the evening before leaving work, we again assembled in front of Mao's portrait. Each person in turn said what they had achieved that day and what "incorrect" ideas had entered their heads.

If you couldn't think of a real self-criticism, you made one up. For instance: "I stumbled earlier today in reciting one of Chairman

Mao's quotations. This shows that I'm not sufficiently loyal to him." Or: "During the criticism session against school president Fan this afternoon, I didn't shout the slogans loudly enough. This shows that my understanding of the class struggle is still weak. Down with capitalist-roader Fan!"

In Beijing, the ritual also had to be repeated at home before going to bed. People knew the neighbours were listening, so they shouted the slogans as loudly as possible. Hua told me later that whenever the family shouted "Long live Chairman Mao," our two-year-old nephew burst into tears, frightened by the noise. One evening, a neighbour peered in through a window to make sure the family was performing. Irritated, Hua yanked open the curtains and ran around turning on all the lights so the nosy neighbour could have a good look.

In the late spring of 1969, Socialist Education Propaganda Teams formed by educated city people were sent to the countryside to "help solve the peasants' problems." In some places, commune leaders, eager to please the central authorities, made a habit of exaggerating how much grain was produced in their area. When production quotas were then set on the basis of these inflated figures, the state inevitably had trouble getting the promised amount of grain from the communes. So trusted people from the cities were sent in to supervise the over-eager rural officials.

A month after my release, Pang was chosen for one such team and sent to a village four hours by train from Harbin. I was left behind, not yet aware that I was pregnant with my second child.

The Red Army had just attacked Zhen Bao Island on the Sino-Soviet border. Our newspapers told us the Russians might invade at any time. Mao issued a directive to "dig tunnels deep and accumulate grain everywhere." Storage pits, where vegetables were kept in winter, were enlarged and turned into makeshift air-raid shelters. Drills were held to help us get used to running into the shelters in an orderly fashion. When winter came, I was heavily pregnant and found it hard to run down the icy stairs and into the pits when the siren sounded. I tried it a couple of times, but then decided I would rather die in the open than be crushed in the pit, or suffocate there, with a baby in my womb.

Some nights we were told to sleep with our clothes on. I thought the Russians were on our doorstep. They never did invade, although we kept digging tunnels. Harbin's ambitious plan was to put concrete and steel supports into the tunnels and link them into a city-wide underground network. Millions of yuan were poured into the project while, above ground, many people had barely enough space to house their families. At our school, families of three or four were allocated only fifteen square metres.

As my pregnancy progressed, I grew more worried about being alone. I cabled Pang, asking him to come home, but he couldn't. He wasn't allowed to come back until two weeks before the baby was due. I wanted the child to be born in Beijing, where my mother could help out after the delivery. Pang couldn't get permission to accompany me on the train, but he did anyway. Later, he lost a month's pay and had to make a self-criticism for this defiance.

Our daughter was born in Beijing on February 28, 1970. We named her Lu, which means precious jade, and everybody called her Lulu. Just as I was about to head back to Harbin after my fifty-six-day maternity leave, I received a notice from the school that both Pang and I would have to go to live in the countryside. Schools were still closed, and many intellectuals were being sent to live with and learn from the peasants. We had no idea how long this period of "re-education" might last. We were to present ourselves within ten days to local officials in Mulan county, about four hours by road from Harbin.

Six couples from our school, all of whom had already suffered in some way during the Cultural Revolution, were being sent to villages in Mulan. Some couples took their young children with them, but we decided it was too risky to take a newborn. There was no pasteurized milk for a bottle-fed baby. What if she got sick? Infant mortality was high in the countryside.

My mother, now in her seventies, was already looking after a baby, my brother's son. Her movements were becoming clumsier and her eyesight weaker, but she still thought she had unlimited resources. "Leave Lulu with me," she insisted. "I can take care of both babies, one on either side of me in the bed at night." But I felt it would be too much for her, and so I found a woman in Beijing who agreed to look after Lulu for fifty yuan a month; quite a bite out of my salary of seventy-eight yuan.

Once again, I had to leave a baby just as she was beginning to recognize my face. Ten years earlier, I had had to leave Yan in Beijing when Wang and I were sent to Harbin. Leaving Lulu behind revived painful memories of that earlier separation. And I found this second one even more wrenching: any hope of finally settling down and being allowed to lead a quiet family life had once again been shattered. At the age of thirty-five this was harder to come to terms with than it had been at twenty-five.

Remembering what life in a village was like, I went back to Harbin loaded with provisions: dried food, noodles, cooking lard, medicine. Pang had been released from his previous assignment and arrived back in Harbin at about the same time. We loaded our few belongings on to a truck and headed for Mulan county before the deadline.

It was a rough ride; the farther we went, the bumpier the road became. When we reached our destination, I was shocked to see the village's mud houses; I had expected brick.

I was sitting up front beside the driver when we pulled into the village. People suddenly appeared from every direction and crowded around the cab of the truck.

"Look! Strangers!" shouted a young boy.

"Look at the woman! She's got glasses," one woman whispered. Peasant whispers were not meant to be inaudible.

"And fat!" said another. I had put on weight, about fifteen pounds, thanks to all the extra food I was allowed after Lulu's birth.

The villagers examined us from head to toe. We looked shabbier than them, with our patched clothing and dirty cloth shoes. We had deliberately dressed like that, because we were under orders to "integrate" with them. Now we saw that most of them were better dressed than we had expected. They told us later they thought we were just pretending to be poor. And they never understood what it was we thought we could learn from them.

Pang and the driver asked the production team leader where we should unload. No one seemed to know. The villagers had not been told we were coming. "If they're not ready for us," I said to the driver, "why don't we just drive back?" He told me to be patient.

While the men went out to try to resolve the mix-up, I stayed in the truck, for several hours. The villagers' first impression of me could not have been a pleasant one: the city woman sitting by herself in the big truck, sulking.

The team leader eventually came back to report that we would be sharing a house with two families. A village house normally has three rooms: you enter through the middle one, in which stoves, water jar, fuel and cooking utensils for both families are kept. The other rooms are off to either side and each is occupied by one family. In the house we were to live in, one room was occupied by a widow and her six children; the other by a widower in his late sixties. In each room, sleeping platforms were built opposite each other along the walls; the space between these two kangs was just wide enough for a table.

We were to share the room with the widower. I hung a sheet up along the side of our kang for a bit of privacy. But we heard the man's every movement during the night: coughing, snoring, urinating. Flies and mosquitoes were a problem and I also rigged up a mosquito net around our kang, which shocked the villagers.

"Look at how much fine gauze she's used to make such a big net. What a waste!" a girl peering in through the door said in a peasant "whisper."

I lay awake the first night, sweltering inside the mosquito net and brooding about my daughters. How long would our separation have to last? I knew Yan was in good hands, living with my sister Wen, but how was a stranger treating Lulu?

The mosquito net, stuffy in the summer heat, was bad enough. But warm air from the evening's cooking also travelled from stove to kang, raising the temperature on the sleeping platform. It was a practical way of keeping it warm in winter, but unbearably hot in summer.

Towards dawn, I sat up in bed. "Pang," I said, "are you awake? I can't stay here."

"I know how you feel," he said, rolling over sleepily to face me. "But where can we go? Our residence permits, ration books, everything, have been transferred here with us. There's no place for us in the city."

I wept in despair. "I can't stand this. We have no idea if Lulu is all right."

"Look, Zhimei," he said softly, "I know how hard it is for you. If you really can't stand it, you can go back to Beijing and look after the baby. I'll stay here by myself."

I knew he was just saying this to comfort me. I knew perfectly well that I had no choice but to stay. If I left, I wouldn't be paid, and we needed my income just to subsist.

The next day, I looked and felt awful. Pang told me to have a rest while he unpacked our things, then lit the small coal stove that we had brought with us. We had even brought half a ton of coal, better fuel, we thought, than the wood and crop stalks the villagers used. Pang started to prepare a meal. Some of the villagers had never seen a man cooking before, and certainly not cooking for his wife. Soon, every villager had heard that "the city woman doesn't know how to cook. Her husband has to do everything for her."

I became the object of great curiosity. People came and went whenever they liked. Some peeped in through the windows; others stood in the doorway and stared at me for hours on end. Some of the bolder ones would ask a few simple questions (such as: "How many children do you have?") and then leave to spread the news.

When the villagers learned that I had left a baby in Beijing, they thought the situation was very cruel. I wished the party was as human as these down-to-earth peasants.

I kept to myself at first, not because I didn't like the villagers, but because I was so unhappy and preoccupied with my own problems. Later, when I got to know them, I liked them a lot. They were genuine and warm and more human in their simple ways than most city people tended to be. They didn't discuss the class struggle and they didn't discriminate against me because of my family background or my divorce. I was just a city woman to them, and it was a relief to be accepted as such.

I joined the women in the fields, doing nearly everything they did: planting, hoeing, weeding, threshing, harvesting, collecting manure and spreading it on the fields. Life is not easy for a peasant woman. She works in the fields, takes care of the children, does all the cooking, mending and sewing, tends her own vegetable plot, and feeds the pigs and poultry. She pumps water from a well, which may be some distance away, and carries it home on a shoulder pole.

When it rained, the village became a sea of mud and there seemed to be sewage everywhere. But I soon got used to the peasant way of life. I came to enjoy their crude humour; I liked their natural food. But I was careful never to drink unboiled water because there were two afflictions prevalent in the area: Keshan disease, which affects the heart, and Kaschin-Beck disease, widespread among young people in northeast China. Its symptoms include aching joints, which are often swollen and deformed, and muscular atrophy. Sufferers are short and some remain dwarfs. The causes were unknown, but some doctors suspected the water in the area had something to do with it.

The six families from our school lived in four neighbouring villages. We met every two weeks for political study. We felt closer to each other than before because we were facing the same problems. We had no idea whether we would ever be allowed back to the city. We all just quietly hoped for a change in policy.

In February 1971, Pang and I received permission to go to Beijing for a few days to see Lulu, now one year old. I burst into tears when I saw her; she was so weak she couldn't sit up on her own, let alone stand. The woman I had left her with had taken advantage of the arrangement and had not fed her properly.

"It's criminal to take food from a child's mouth," my mother said. We searched for another caretaker and found one in an older woman who loved children. Lulu would be much better treated now, but I returned to the countryside consumed with guilt that I was not able to give her the motherly love and care she deserved.

During our second year in the village, Pang and I moved to a room near the well. A bean curd workshop was opposite our room and the middle room, where our stove stood, contained a large soy bean mill. It was operated by a blinkered donkey, who walked round and round the room, dumping dung along the way. As I sat fanning the fire in our stove, his tail would sometimes swish against my face. But I didn't mind. At least now we had some privacy.

I learned a lot about the village from an old hunchback who would arrive before daybreak to make bean curd. He knew all the gossip. One family, he said, had drowned a deformed baby in the cesspool; another was rife with incest; a dwarf in the village (called Big Guy, of course) loved to gamble; and so on.

Pang got involved in one of the village's more horrifying episodes. Early one morning, an agitated neighbour knocked at the door: "Pang! Get up! Two people have been murdered!"

Pang threw on his coat and rushed out. When he arrived on the scene, dozens of people were clustered around the village well. He pushed through the crowd and saw a man's head bobbing above the water. "Throw him a rope!" Pang shouted.

"Leave me alone! I want to die," the man in the well pleaded.

"You're a coward!" Pang yelled down the well. "If you had wanted to die, why didn't you do it properly and jump in head first?" Pang threw the man a rope and he climbed out, with difficulty, because his padded clothes were waterlogged. He was trembling violently.

It was Gui, who had married a widow with two teenage daughters. But he had become more interested in the older daughter than the mother. Incest is not unusual in the countryside, where two or even three generations sleep in the same room, spread out on two facing kangs.

Gui made a habit of sleeping with the girl. But when a boy in the village wanted to marry her, the girl pleaded with Gui to end their own disgraceful relationship. When he refused, she told her mother everything. Gui flew into a rage, raped and strangled the girl, and killed the mother with a cleaver. He wrapped the two corpses neatly in padded quilts, then walked to the well and threw himself in. He was arrested and, we heard, severely beaten by police. Six months later, he pleaded guilty and was executed.

In the spring of 1972, with the worst of the Cultural Revolution turmoil over, universities began to reopen. Of the six couples sent from our school to Mulan county, half were to be allowed back to Harbin to resume teaching. We were told to decide among ourselves who should go and who stay. Pang insisted I should be among the first to return to the city; he himself would have to stay on for six more months.

And so, after a six-year absence, I was back in the classroom. I was assigned to the English department of Heilongjiang University, popularly known as Heida. The composition of the student body was quite different now. Workers, peasants, and soldiers recommended by their work units and communes filled the universities. Entrance exams were abolished, because they were viewed as a means for bourgeois intellectuals to oppress the proletariat. We teachers had to be extra careful about how we treated our students: if we ever showed impatience or gave poor marks, we could be accused of class vengeance.

Before I resumed teaching, I went to Beijing to collect Lulu. She was two years old and barely knew me. It was a while before she called me Ma. It was even harder for her to get used to a Pa. We were assigned one room, where we lived for the next seven years.

At first we had only one bed, which caused some drama on Pang's first night back in Harbin. Lulu woke up in the night, saw a man beside her and began to wail. I tried to comfort her, but she kept pushing Pang, wanting him off the bed.

"Why don't you go and sit in the chair until she falls asleep and then crawl back in?" I suggested.

"I don't want to upset her. I'll sleep on the floor tonight." And so, after being separated as a family for two years, Pang spent our reunion on the floor.

When Pang and I were sent to Mulan county, my sister Wen had also been banished to the countryside. Yan went with her and attended the local village school for her last three years of primary school. Having lived with Wen since she was six, Yan was close to her and called us both Ma. She felt equally at home, living with me or my sister.

We all agreed that Yan would be better off in a city school for her secondary education, so she came to live with us in 1973. The next few years were a peaceful patch, during which there were no major disruptions to family life. Pang and I lived amicably. Yan and Lulu got to know each other for the first time; with a ten-year age gap, there was no rivalry between them.

When Wen was finally allowed to return to Hefei from the countryside in 1976, Yan went back to live with her. It was Yan's decision. She knew that her second "Ma," who had recently divorced, would be lonely living on her own.

Chapter Eleven

LIFE IN THE PRESENT TENSE

Jin strode into the classroom wearing a severe expression above his tightly fastened Mao jacket. My fellow teachers and I fell silent, startled by the early appearance this year of the wool overcoat draped over his shoulders. It was late August, 1977; surely Jin would roast in his coat in the stuffy, sun-drenched room. But he was fond of the look considered chic by many party officials who were former army officers: an overcoat hanging from the shoulders lent him, he felt, a commanding air.

As head of the school's Foreign Affairs Office, Jin had called a mandatory staff meeting to discuss the imminent arrival of a new foreign teacher. He sat down at the front of the room, and flipped through the pages of a thick file. He stopped and frowned at one entry in what I assumed was a dossier on the foreigner.

Heilongjiang University had had foreign teachers before, two British couples in succession. But the new foreigner was arousing more than the usual interest because it was rumoured that he was Jewish-Canadian and his wife, Hispanic-American. Foreigners were rarities in Harbin, let alone such exotic ones. What would their children look like? And why was the man's dossier already so thick?

"The new foreigner speaks Chinese," Jin began. "His name is Daniel Levy and he'll be arriving in a few days with his wife, Marta, and two young children, Rosa and Josh. He studied Chinese for a couple of years in Beijing and so he feels comfortable living in China." He turned a page and cleared his throat. Jin's important points were always introduced by a prolonged gurgling of phlegm.

"It also says here that he likes to get close to Chinese, that he'll appear at your home unannounced and walk right in without any formality. This has got to be watched. We'll have to be extra vigilant with this foreign guest, careful never to forget the distinction between *nei* and *wai*." By invoking the principle of "inside versus outside," Jin was repeating a warning we had heard countless times before: "inside information" must be guarded from foreigners.

My first contact with the newcomers came about a week later, as I was walking back from teaching my first class of the new school year. A small girl in a navy blue jumpsuit was hovering at the edge of a dusty courtyard in the residential section of campus. Long dark hair was coiled in a neat bun on top of her head. She was watching shyly as a group of girls played high-speed skipping games with elastic jump ropes.

"Hello, Rosa," I said, and saw her face relax. She had been straining to make sense of the babble around her and clearly was relieved to be addressed in her own language. "I'm a teacher just like your dad. And I have a daughter who's a bit older than you." Big brown eyes stared up at me. "Where do you live?" she asked. I pointed to the building opposite theirs.

"Can I go and see your daughter's toys?"

It was strictly forbidden to let a foreigner into your home without permission from school authorities. On the other hand, how could I refuse a small girl who only wanted a look at the toys this strange new land had to offer?

Still, I reacted with instinctive caution. "You can meet my daughter Lulu when she comes home from school."

"Let's go *now*," she said, and took my hand. I smiled at her boldness and relented.

My neighbours sitting around the doorway of our building looked on in surprise as we headed up to my room on the second floor. Rosa ran a hand along the walls of the stairwell and it was soon coated in grime. We cooked on coal stoves in the corridors, and the walls were a permanent greasy grey.

The first thing that caught Rosa's eye at the top of the stairs was our five leghorn hens. Pang had built a wooden coop for them with material scavenged from a construction site. We kept the coop's small hinged door locked to prevent hens and eggs being stolen. Lulu's nourishment depended on our homegrown eggs, the only protein supplementing our monthly ration of 250 grams of meat per person and eight eggs per family.

Nearly every household kept a coop, and as we whiled away winter evenings chatting with our neighbours in the corridor, the conversation often turned to the care and feeding of hens. One of the discoveries I passed on was that my hens loved to eat newsprint. I didn't tell my neighbours that I also fed the hens my personal correspondence. "Now you know all my secrets," I whispered to the hungry hens as I watched my shredded letters disappear. "But I don't think any of you will betray me."

I fed them the letters I received from Sarah and Bob, a British couple who had taught at the school. But by the time their letters reached me, they had already been opened by the humourless bunch in the school's Foreign Affairs Office, who also read my out-going mail. When Sarah asked in a letter whether I was able to "decode" a note from Bob, Jin leapt on that suspect word and demanded an explanation. I said that Sarah was obviously referring to Bob's poor handwriting, but Jin was not convinced.

In one of my letters to Sarah, I mentioned a funny mistake made by a foreigner just beginning to learn Chinese. I had gone with the woman, a new teacher at the school, to buy some powdered milk. She was eager to practise her first words of Chinese, but got the tones wrong and ended up asking for "cow dung," causing the shop assistant to giggle.

I was summoned to the Foreign Affairs Office. "I think you should cross that part out," Jin said, pointing to the offending anecdote in my letter. "This sort of talk is not serious. Don't write in this frivolous way in future." After a while I got tired of having to participate in this censorship and I stopped writing letters to Britain. The hens went back on a more restricted diet of People's Daily editorials.

Rosa didn't see much worth investigating in our simply furnished room. "Run downstairs and play in the sand," I said, and gave her a plastic shovel and pail. She skipped downstairs in a much cheerier mood.

Later, as I was putting on my apron to cook dinner, I heard a knock at the door. It was Rosa, hand-in-hand with her mother, a dark, attractive woman in T-shirt and bell-bottoms. Her hair was tucked up in a kerchief. I couldn't tell how old she was; it was hard to guess a foreigner's age.

"This is the woman I talked to, Mommy!" Rosa said.

I had already broken the rules when I brought Rosa to my place, but the risks hadn't seemed serious when the foreigner involved stood three feet tall. Should I invite this grown foreigner in? The decision was made for me as the woman eased into the room.

"Hi, my name is Marta. My daughter said she'd met a Chinese woman who speaks English. My husband suggested I go find out who you were. So here I am. Hope I'm not disturbing you."

I was nervous, both because of the rule being broken as we spoke and because of the stark simplicity of our room. It held a wardrobe, two beds, a bookshelf and desk. The table that we ate on was folded up and leaning against a wall beside the small window. The room looked so uncomfortable when I saw it through a foreigner's eyes, and I mumbled an apology.

"Don't be silly," she said. "You know, I was brought up poor in New York and our furniture was always very plain. My sister and I shared a single bed the whole time we were growing up."

I was taken with her openness and began to feel more relaxed.

But I was still relieved when, after a few minutes, she said they had to get going.

First thing next morning I went to the Foreign Affairs Office to explain that I hadn't invited her to my room. School officials were supposed to inspect your room and the communal corridors before deciding if they were clean enough to receive foreign guests.

Jin was in the office when I entered. He had been expecting me. "I'm glad you came to make this report," he said. "It is, of course, important to maintain good relations with our foreign teachers." He cleared his throat. "But keep in mind that we don't yet know this couple's political attitude. As long as you know what you should and shouldn't say to them, you'll be OK."

The next day, the English department held a party to welcome Daniel and Marta, five-year-old Rosa and seven-year-old Josh. The event was held in the same classroom in which, just a week before, we had been given the warning about Daniel. This time, a long table set up at the front held tea cups and thermos bottles, plates of sunflower seeds, peanuts and candies. The Levys sat in the middle, flanked by members of the Foreign Affairs Office and the deans of the English department. Jin made sure the foreigners' tea cups were kept full and from time to time placed a handful of sunflower seeds in front of them.

The head of the English department made his standard speech for welcoming foreigners to the school: "... friendship ... friendly co-operation ... friends of China ..." The only variation this time was a reference to Norman Bethune, "who also travelled thousands of miles to help the Chinese people." Daniel stared hard at his pipe, uncomfortable at being compared to the only Canadian known to most Chinese – the Montreal surgeon who died in China in 1939 while tending communist troops.

Then came Daniel's turn. I was transfixed by the sight of him. I had never seen a man with such long hair before: his dark curly hair touched his shoulders. He was tall and slim and bearded, and wore a light-coloured shirt and jeans. He puffed on a pipe as he talked about the deep feelings for China he had developed during his two years as a student in Beijing.

Then he halted, knocked the ashes out of his pipe, and said: "There's a wall around our building. Is it there to keep us in or to keep the Chinese out?"

A shocked silence fell. The cracking of sunflower seeds ceased. Daniel sat down, and instead of the usual polite round of applause, the Foreign Affairs cadres just looked embarrassed. The awkward little welcoming party was over.

Daniel's job was to improve the English of the school's English teachers. I wasn't among the dozen teachers selected for his first session, but I often slipped into the class and tried to make myself inconspicuous at the back of the room. Daniel obviously liked teaching. He was animated in class, encouraging students to ask questions and speak up whenever they had something to say. He dressed casually, in black corduroy pants and a red-and-black checked shirt unbuttoned at the collar. Beside him, we looked so clumsy and shapeless with baggy blue or grey padded trousers, jackets buttoned to the neck, and not a speck of colour in our clothes.

His manner was as relaxed as his dress. He sat on an empty desk when talking to the class; he wiped the dust off his desk with his sleeve. He drew his students out, so that none would try to remain invisible. His informal style and teaching methods were worlds away from the rote learning to which we were accustomed.

I was a serious auditor; I took notes and did all the written assignments. The theme of our first composition was "An Unusual Experience." I wrote about my two years in East Berlin in the early 1950s. I got the essay back with Daniel's comments: "Excellent. Your descriptions are vivid and there is strong emotional feeling throughout." I was thrilled.

On "What do you think about when you look at the stars?," I wrote about how, as a child, I used to search the sky for the first star to make a wish. "But now I look no more at stars; nor do I pin my hope on their power. Now they are nothing but natural luminous bodies twinkling in the sky, cold and lifeless."

Daniel was obviously taken aback by the tone. "Technically, it is well written," he wrote. "Emotionally it becomes depressing, a little morbid, especially coming from one who so often laughs and expresses pleasure. There's a dark side to Madame Zhang, eh?"

The teachers enrolled in Daniel's class did not like others to audit. They said having extra people in the room was a distraction, even though there were only four of us. We were told we could no longer attend, but I ignored the decision. I thought as many people as possible should benefit from having a foreign teacher on campus, considering that the state paid thousands of yuan to bring each one over. But I soon received a note from Liu, the school's party secretary: "It is the party's decision that no one should audit the class." There was no room for bargaining.

My turn to enrol in Daniel's class came during his third six-month session, in the autumn of 1978. Besides our regular composition assignments, he asked us to write a page in a diary every day to be handed in on Friday. He would return it on Monday, with comments. Our everyday routine was a triangular trip around campus: home, classroom, office, home. There was little novelty in our lives, apart from the resident foreigners. They were thus a favourite topic of conversation, but I could hardly record the gossip about them in a diary to be read by Daniel. There was nothing much that was interesting in the world around me to write about, so I filled the diary with thoughts and reminiscences. Daniel's comments were always encouraging.

When the subject of divorce came up in class, I wrote about my own divorce, about attitudes towards marriage and separation in Chinese culture and how my own strayed from the norm.

"In most cases," I wrote, "the men deserted the women. But in my case, I was the one who wanted out. If spiritually you are not one, what's the sense of being together physically? Society found my behaviour unacceptable: the authorities put pressure on me, colleagues sneered, friends kept their distance. I was left in complete insecurity to face the disgrace, but I withstood it. I took my two-year-old daughter and my belongings and left without asking for child support. Just give me my freedom."

When Daniel handed our diaries back, I opened mine to find one neatly written sentence at the bottom of the page: "An important story waits to be told." I read the line again and again. No one had ever encouraged me to write before.

The diary was becoming more than just language practice; it was another world that I could enter to escape a drab reality. Daniel's enthusiasm for my writing, his supportive comments, made me want to tell him more. It was a wild fantasy to imagine I could ever really write my life story. Nevertheless, I decided to abandon the rambling essays on assorted topics I had been writing and try my hand at autobiography.

I had a sense the diary was becoming something special for Daniel, too – a window on to China and Chinese attitudes. I was energized by the interest he showed, and eager to convey to this sympathetic foreigner something of the texture of a Chinese life.

Near the end of term, he asked us to prepare a book report. Most of the teachers discussed pedagogical texts or other serious academic works. I alone chose a Western novel, *Papillon* by Henri Charrière, who was himself Papillon, so named because of a butterfly tattooed on his chest, a symbol of his obsession with freedom. I desperately wanted to do well, so I wrote my talk down word for word and made sure to look up all unfamiliar words in the book, such as "stool pigeon" and "dungeon."

I also wanted to look my best for the presentation and thought a new haircut was in order. But an absent-minded hairdresser cut my hair several inches shorter than I had requested. I thought I looked ridiculous, like a severe, old-fashioned schoolteacher, and when I walked into the classroom the next morning I wished I could tug my hair longer.

In the first part of my presentation I traced the story of a man who had made eight daring but unsuccessful escapes from Devil's Island and succeeded on his ninth try. No one had ever made it off the island alive before. In the second part, I discussed what I understood to be the book's central themes. On the one hand, the story was an indictment of the injustice of the French penal system; it was also, I said, "a vivid portrayal of the unconquerable forces of integrity and courage that had allowed a wronged man to prevail in the end."

"How should we look at a person's past and future?" I asked, introducing the final segment of my talk. "Isn't it true that in some places the view that 'once a thief, always a thief' or 'a thief's child is also a thief' is still alive and well, and that many are suffering the consequences? No one is ever lost for good. They must be given a chance to become honest. But it's not easy to step out of chains you've been dragging around for years, or to erase a label you've been wearing all your life."

"Any questions?" I asked. No one said a word. The silence was ominous. Daniel, who was sitting at my desk with his legs stretched out into the aisle, just kept tapping his pen on the desk and nodding slowly, deep in thought. "Well done," he said finally, getting up to give me back my seat.

The woman sitting beside me whispered: "You have guts. I like that." Another leaned forward to whisper: "Aren't you worried you'll be reported?" But I didn't care. I had never dared to state my thoughts so openly before and I felt I had done it cleverly, in the guise of a book report. And, I discovered, it was an enormous relief to speak my mind.

The semester was drawing to a close. Since we all enjoyed the class so much, we asked for an extension, but the deans refused. And party secretary Liu called a teachers' meeting.

"The classroom," he said, "is a battleground of the class struggle. We should never let it be dominated by bourgeois ideas. And so we should guard against the imperceptible influence the foreign teacher has on our thinking. Some of our teachers are unaware of this." He raised his voice as he warmed to the topic. "But, more seriously, a few have willingly allowed themselves to be led on by a foreigner." Everyone knew who he meant.

Our session with Daniel ended, my classwork with him was finished, but my homework continued. I still wrote many pages in a diary every week and gave them to him for comments. I wrote in a looseleaf binder, so I could take out the previous week's pages and keep them somewhere safe at home. This way, if the diary ever fell into the wrong hands, only a few pages would be read.

Week after week, I recounted episodes from my childhood, from schooldays at Sacred Heart, from my two marriages, from the Cultural Revolution. Daniel and I communicated in this way for many months. Over time, the contents and tone of my entries and his replies became more personal. Slowly it dawned on me that I was falling in love. Here I was, a forty-four-year-old woman in her second marriage and I had never known the feeling. Although I was fond of Pang, and appreciated his unwavering support and affection, I had never been in love with him.

In a situation in which even casual contact between Chinese and foreigners was restricted, an intimate relationship with Daniel was completely out of the question. Moreover, we were both married, and he was ten years my junior. The whole thing was unthinkable, and unstoppable.

We created opportunities to see each other, even if it was just a glimpse from a distance. I jogged every morning, and he did Tai Chi inside his fenced-off yard. The surreptitious exchange of a smile as I ran slowly past became a daily ritual. If for some reason one of us couldn't make that silent morning rendez-vous, we both felt something was missing from the day. Once he stepped on a nail and couldn't exercise for more than a week. But he would appear on his balcony to watch me run past and wave if he thought no one was watching. Once he blew a kiss and I almost stumbled. We were nourished by these little things.

One summer evening, as I was coming home from teaching a

night class, I saw Daniel in the distance leaving my building. I called to him, but he didn't seem to hear.

I was barely in the door when there came a knock. It was Daniel. We were in each other's arms before we had even closed the door. I nudged it shut and locked it; Pang and Lulu would both be home soon. Then I was back in Daniel's embrace. It was the first time I had ever really enjoyed being kissed.

"Did you hear me call to you?" I asked.

"Yes. But I couldn't answer, it would have been too obvious. There were so many people sitting outside. I walked on a bit, but couldn't resist coming back."

We held each other a while longer. Before leaving, Daniel whispered in my ear: "Let's proceed, slowly and cautiously."

When I walked into the office the next morning, he was there chatting with other teachers. He was wearing a new pink shirt and looked radiant. Apparently I looked different, too. One of the teachers said: "Look at Zhimei. She's all lit up today! What's up?"

"Well," I stammered, "I got my bonus pay last night. Isn't that great?" I lowered my head to try to hide the blush I could feel colouring my cheeks.

During the break, I went into Daniel's office to get a book, and a moment alone with him.

"Why did you blush when Fan spoke to you?" he said softly. "You're giving yourself away."

One of Daniel's students burst into the room to hand in an assignment. We had been so absorbed that we hadn't heard his footsteps. Daniel's office was too public for the things we now had to say to each other. The diary was as private a place to communicate as we were likely to find. My attempts at autobiography abandoned, our love letters soon filled its pages. Life in the present tense pushed the past away.

I kept only a few of the diary entries we wrote to each other over the next few months. The earliest was dated July 13, 1979, and written by Daniel:

Darling Zhimei, to tell you the truth, I thought that if I just touched a Chinese woman in an improper place, by accident, through five layers of winter clothes, I would have been arrested as a rapist, home-wrecker, bourgeois lust-filled foreign devil. I expected to have my advances rejected so I made no effort.

Love is a force that too many people seem to have forgotten, especially in China. When human love becomes a contemptible kind of sentimentality, and that is what it has been made into in China, it is no wonder that people are so puzzled by it. Love the party, love the army, love the proletarian dictatorship, love Chairman Mao, love anything but another person. How could the people most experienced in love in the whole world be reduced to such a sterile state? Some day the crimes against humanity that were carried out in the name of revolution will be exposed.

I think I know when I first wanted you. It was during the semester you were in my class and I discovered how unique, fresh and free your ideas are. You *are* different from the other women. If you weren't, I wouldn't be doing what I'm doing with you.

You're crazy. I'm insane. China is mad and our love is demented. I feel neither guilt nor shame and if I were not crazy I would feel both. We all go mad in our own way, in our quiet little places, in the dusty, forgotten corners of our meagre minds. Turn your crazy head to pleasure!

Dearest Daniel: My old friend Zhen is very attuned to the vibrations between men and women. She and I also have a lot in common. So she can't understand why the men who appeal to me are so different from the ones who appeal to her.

Three of us were sitting in the staff room today discussing you. They know that I quite like you, but that's all. Zhen said she would never trust a man like you, but I trust you more than anybody else. Lin said you're not a one-woman man. Both of them say you're a smooth-talker and that it's not possible to tell when you're being sincere and when not.

They may be right. It *is* difficult to tell, but not impossible. I can tell.

Then there's my friend Didi, who once said to me: "You've been loved by many people. You know the happiness of being loved, but not the pain of loving, for you have never really loved a man." And she was right. Of all the love others have lavished on me, there has not been much reciprocation on my part. I have not felt love's reverberations, I have not felt disturbed. But with you it's different. I understand now what she meant by pain; maybe agony is a better word for it.

Agony is the word for it, Zhimei. Love is agony. Love is hunger: a burning, insatiable demon that twists and cuts and demands satisfaction. The first love is the hardest to bear. Isn't it amazing how you can feel so good and so miserable at the same time?

It's interesting that the women you relate to most are the ones I find most attractive here. Is it the unhappiness of your lives that I'm so sensitive to? Maybe it's your somewhat non-Chinese attitudes toward life.

I fully understand Zhen's anti-male feelings and enjoy jousting verbally with her. I like her, but could never love her.

Lin is the free spirit who suggests a completely amoral and irresponsible existence. It is appealing but it soon becomes meaningless. I like her, but could never love her.

Then there's Didi, the hopeless romantic; the dreams she cast aside would fill the universe. She carries a sadness about her that arouses too much sympathy in me. I like her, but could never love her.

I perform for them because they are an appreciative audience. With you it is something special and private. You see through me; you know so much without being told. You say you want a place in my heart? Zhimei, you will have a palace in my soul.

But is there such a thing as a one-woman man? There is a one-man woman; why not the other? Maybe this is one of the ways that men are different. It is an ancient, animal behaviour. You *are* made for me and I do love you, but never just you alone. Love cannot be that limited.

Dear Daniel, an awful thing happened yesterday. Hou dropped by to see whether I'd recovered from my cold. Do you think he came out of concern for one of his staff? No. He wanted to be alone with me: "I miss you when you're not in the office. You're different from other women."

"You shouldn't be saying this," I said. "We're both married." He said his wife can't satisfy his emotional needs. I would have told him to clear off immediately, if he weren't my boss. Then he showed his animal side. He leapt at me and nearly tore my clothes off. I struggled and yelled. See the behaviour of a party member? He left disappointed, but still assuming a superior air. He knew I wouldn't report him because people would believe him, not me. Or I would be accused of seducing him.

Dearest Zhimei, I think the men around here have been living in such a sterile environment for so long that they're starved for good, healthy, natural and sincere woman vibes.

Hunger makes one's sense of smell more acute. The men are approaching male menopause and feeling surges of hormones and reflecting on the past. I think the change in you is obvious; your women friends can sense it, too, but no one can explain it except us two.

You must be more forceful in repelling the veiled and obvious attacks that may occur. Silent suffering and brooding will only attract a new attack.

Daniel, Jin has told us you've extended your contract for another year. But I know Marta has no interest in staying longer. She often says things to me like: "I've given up too much for Daniel. I want something of my own now." She seems to fear the longer she stays in China, the more difficult it will be to get back into your own society. Don't you feel the same way?

There are some touchy things I've tried to ignore, but I know I'll have to face them sooner or later. It would be dishonest of me to say I haven't taken anything from Marta. But I hope I haven't taken too much, so that I can feel less guilty.

My darling Zhimei, the job I have now is the first one I've ever really enjoyed, especially since I feel that I'm doing something constructive with my time. I never had that feeling in Canada. Life seemed to be an empty chase for material accumulation and electronically supplied thrills. One becomes addicted to consumerism, a mad consumerism that becomes an end in itself. Here, I'm still a consumer, but of experiences, not things. Simple is better in life and more in tune with my nature.

Marta has often said that China suits me fine, but doesn't suit her. I'm being selfish, expecting her to live according to my style. At some point everyone's selfishness manifests itself in some way. We have reached a critical point in the marriage where compromise seems reasonable, and yet undesirable.

For the past year, both of us have sensed the diminishing of common ground between us. China does that to a lot of people. I suppose living in China does a lot to sharpen different attitudes towards life. Marta cannot understand why I like China so much, especially since she likes it so little. I have a friend who likes to remind me that Jews can live anywhere.

Having met you has strengthened my feeling that it might be possible to dissolve a marriage, not in anger, but with love and understanding. You see, people can be in love and still want to divorce. Because isn't it better to realize the differences before the relationship becomes destructive? A bitter divorce can destroy both partners and is especially damaging to children.

Marta and I haven't committed ourselves to divorce, but we talk about it more now and with less anxiety. One of the strongest forces working against divorce is what other people will think. It is generally considered a failure in marriage. Better to admit failure after thirteen years than live with it until death.

Dear Daniel: You say that living in China has sharpened the differences between you and Marta. What would have become of your marriage if you hadn't come to China? Will the differences between you disappear again quietly, much as they arose?

Maybe your marriage will be like my own: knowing there's no way to change it, I just let it stay in a holding pattern: no improvement and no deterioration. But there's always been a lot of understanding between Pang and me. I hope this time, when it comes to giving me up, he will be as understanding as he has always been. I must tell him the truth.

Zhimei, my wife has been a giver all her life. I am both giver and taker, though with her it has been mostly take. What do you expect? When you live with a giver you take. Now Marta feels she's been a fool all these years. Her friends and relatives call her a fool; even my own brothers call her a fool. And she has come to believe it.

I want total devotion from a woman. I don't want a slave, though. I want spirit and initiative, too. No woman I've ever met has given me such a thrill as you have. Perhaps you are endowed with the direct opposite of the force within me.

So here we are, twenty years late for you and thirteen years late for me. Can the saying "better late than never" be applied here? Every day I think of more and more reasons why it can.

Having perceived the fierce spirit still burning in you, I could not bear to let it die. I could not leave it to smother in the oppressive atmosphere of this place. My love was aroused, a love of something beautiful. For I love freedom, freedom from morality, from politics, from responsibility . . . amoral, apolitical, irresponsible.

Are you sure you want to come with me? I'm sure I want to take you. No matter how much I've given China (not much), it will never equal what I take when I leave. China loses a beautiful, creative, spirited, thinking woman. When I take, I take a lot.

The future holds much uncertainty for both of us. But you survived uncertainty during dark days and you will survive again. You are a survivor.

Chapter Twelve

BREAK FOR FREEDOM

Two years after Daniel's arrival at Heida, the topic of divorce was on the agenda both for me and Pang, and for Daniel and Marta. I wasn't sure I could do it. I knew how much Pang wanted to keep the family intact for the sake of our daughter. He adored Lulu and didn't want her to have even a taste of what he had suffered as a child, raised by his alcoholic grandfather.

In August 1979, Pang, Lulu and I were assigned a two-room apartment in a new teachers' dormitory, a fifteen-minute walk from Daniel's building. Even during Yan's three years in Harbin, the four of us had had to share one room and we weren't sorry to leave it.

The new building's small pump was not powerful enough to propel water up to the third floor, so we had to carry it up from downstairs for cooking, washing and flushing the toilet. But this seemed a minor inconvenience. It was the first apartment I had ever had and I luxuriated in having all that private space.

Pang and I had been sleeping separately for some time, and we agreed I would have my own room in the new apartment. At the time, Lulu was closer to Pang than to me. The bigger of the two rooms had two single beds, for Pang and for Lulu. My room was tiny, and cold in winter because the building was not well heated. But once I closed my bedroom door, it felt cosy in there. I had never had such privacy in which to write the diary.

I was madly in love with Daniel. To me, he was the epitome of intelligence, wit, strength, pleasure, freedom, and hope. He represented everything I wanted and didn't have: a world where people could follow their hearts, and speak their minds without fear; where they could be themselves and make their own decisions. He brought information about the world outside China from which we were isolated. He encouraged me to learn and to express myself freely, and I gained self-confidence. He had a sense of humour I found missing among Chinese. He gave me spiritual and physical pleasure I had never experienced before.

At the same time, there was an element of mystery about him because he was, after all, a Westerner, so different from us. In the same way, Asian women hold a powerful attraction for many Western men, and Chinese officials' attempt to discourage relationships only adds to the allure.

Daniel saw in me a free spirit much like himself who was ready to unveil the mysteries of China and of its women, and he was unable to resist. With me, he was adored and trusted to a degree he had never been before. What we got from each other, what we represented to each other, was like a powerful drug, and it made us feel certain we could overcome all obstacles to be together.

It was, of course, a painful subject to broach with Pang. My husband had never wronged me in any way; he had only ever loved me. But I had to be honest with him. I owed him that much. We had a talk one evening after Lulu was asleep.

"I don't think we should go on living like this," I said. "I can't go on . . . cheating you, and myself."

"I've been expecting this," Pang said sadly. "I've also realized we've drifted apart. What do you have in mind?"

"I want a divorce. I want a life of my own."

Pang was struggling to keep his cool. "Who do you want to be with?" he said at last. "Is it . . . ?" His hands gripped the edge of his chair.

"Yes." We both knew who I meant. Many people around us had

sensed a bond between Daniel and myself. How could I expect Pang not to have noticed?

He got up suddenly, went over to the window and stood with his back to me. I was afraid he was going to explode at any moment. The minutes he stood there, stock-still and silent, were excruciating. Only the ticking of a clock broke the silence. He poured himself a cup of tea and walked back to his seat. The look on his face startled me; it was cold and expressionless.

He heaved a deep sigh. "Tell me what your plan is."

"I want to marry him."

"Do you know what kind of risk you're taking? You realize you're breaking the rules? Don't forget that both of you are married. He can get away with it because he's a foreigner, but you can't. You could be accused of anything."

Pang was alluding to what was, in fact, my greatest fear. There had been cases before of Chinese being expelled from their workplaces or sent to labour camps because they had become involved with foreigners. My case was the first of its kind in Harbin. If it came to the attention of officials, we, or rather I, would be in deep trouble. I knew that as well as Pang, but I was ready to take the risk. Now it was my turn for silence. I stared at the floor.

"Why don't you answer me?" he said. "Aren't you afraid that I might report you?"

Now I looked him in the eye: "I don't think you'd do that to me. You've never done anything to harm me. You've only ever loved and protected me. Do you think I don't appreciate that?"

Pang said nothing, and so I continued. "Remember what you said when we got married? You said you hoped our marriage would save us both. If you ruin me now, you will also be ruining yourself and Lulu. You know how it is – if one fish stinks, the whole pot of fish stinks. I don't want to ruin you. I'm just asking for my freedom. We both know that neither of us finds this marriage very satisfying. Can't you do this one last thing for me? It may be totally selfish of me to ask this of you, but I want my freedom so badly."

Pang now looked more sad than threatening. "Do you know what disgrace I'll have to face and what pressure I'll be under if this becomes public? I know you've been unhappy and I knew this would come up sooner or later. But I didn't expect you to get involved with a foreigner. How far can you trust a foreigner? Do you think he's really serious about you?"

"I'm certain he's serious. He loves me. He thinks I'm endowed with the direct opposite of the force within him and that we are made for each other."

I was quoting Daniel's own words. I was so in love with him that I revered his every word and believed him utterly. If the declarations of love he wrote in the diary had been written in Chinese, I don't think I would have found them so moving. But, written in a foreign language, they had greater mystique.

"From all the books you've read," Pang said, "I'd have thought you might have noticed that most Western men are not faithful to their wives. Don't you know that in the West there's no such thing as a one-woman man? Don't you know that all men, especially Western men, like younger women? Do you mean to tell me he's ready to give up a wife his own age to marry someone ten years older? Be reasonable, Zhimei. And don't forget that Marta is the woman he has lived with for thirteen years. Those ties are not easy to cut. You're in a position of secondary importance."

I knew there were no guarantees, and that our destinies were not in our own hands. Daniel and I had made a verbal commitment which could only be met if two other people agreed to the changes.

"I survived the tortures of the past," I said. "I'll certainly survive the uncertainties of the future." Again, I borrowed Daniel's words.

"I've said all I should say and asked all I should ask," Pang said. "If it's really what you want, I'll give you your freedom. I'm thinking more of you than of him. I know what potential you have, and that it will never be fulfilled if you stay here. Because of your past, you'll never get fair treatment. I can't bear to see you being smothered."

I was in tears. It was only then that I fully appreciated how much Pang loved me and how unselfishly he was prepared to sacrifice himself for me. I was never as affectionate with him as I was that night. He stayed the night with me in my bed. We talked and talked, and clung to each other like a pair of love-birds. Our marriage was going to end but a deeper understanding had developed between us.

We discussed the most painful point: Lulu. We decided that she would have a better chance in life if she stayed with me, assuming I did make it to Canada with Daniel. Pang was devoted to his daughter, but he knew that my background could blight her own future in China. We agreed there would be no child support and no division of possessions. I wanted only my own clothes and books.

The next day, I confided in my friend Zhen. She had suspected my relationship with Daniel was intimate, but I had never confirmed it for her. Now I poured out the whole story.

"You're lucky to have such an understanding husband, Zhimei. No man will ever do as much for you as Pang has done, and so unconditionally. In the same situation, I think my husband would rather see me miserable than let me go."

Zhen and her husband didn't get along. She had had a boyfriend before they met; that bothered her husband and he never let her forget it. They divorced after a few unhappy years, but, during the Cultural Revolution, Zhen agreed to remarry him. Now she viewed that decision as the biggest mistake of her life.

"What do you think of Daniel, Zhen?"

"In all honesty, he's not my type. I don't trust him. I know he likes your brains, but remember, Western men put a lot of importance on a woman's physical appearance, and you are quite a bit older. But tell me, Zhimei, are you really in love with him or is he just a plane ticket out of China?"

"I've never felt this kind of love before. I don't care where he is, here or abroad, I want to be with him."

"In that case, I envy you and I hope he'll treat you well." We held each other, and I noticed Zhen's eyes were moist when she spoke again.

"We're a lot alike, Zhimei. We've both felt the lack of romance in our lives; it's just that you're more courageous than me in seeking it out. Whenever I see couples holding hands in the street, or kissing in the movies, my heart aches and I have to look away." Such an affectionate and passionate woman – it was so unfair! Zhen and I had often wondered how many couples actually married for love. Looking around us, we saw very few.

The next step was to get permission from the school for the divorce and for me to move to Beijing. I wanted to leave Harbin before the scandal of my relationship with Daniel broke. First, I asked for the transfer; hardly a strange request, because I had asked for the same thing several times before. My longing to return to Beijing was well known, but I had always been refused.

Party secretary Liu, usually dour, was smiling when he appeared one morning in the teachers' office. "Comrade Zhang, I've read your application. Would you come to my office?"

In his office, he sat in a leather armchair behind a huge desk, and I sat opposite. I knew this was the moment of truth.

"I see that you want to leave us," Liu said, glancing at my two-page application. "You've contributed a lot to the school, and we'll be sorry to see you go. If you think it's time you left we won't do anything to stop you this time. But you'll have to find a work unit in Beijing that will accept you."

I was surprised, and thrilled, that without the slightest hesitation he had finally accepted my application to leave.

"Don't be naive, Zhimei," Zhen said when I told her my good news. "The department has figured out something's going on between you and Daniel. They want to get rid of you before your case is officially out in the open and causes them trouble."

I didn't care what their motives were. I just wanted to leave. In order to marry Daniel, I would have to leave my husband, my job and my friends in Harbin. Now I was one step closer.

I immediately wrote to Hua, who was teaching at a school in Beijing, and asked her about job possibilities. Her reply was encouraging: "My school is looking for English teachers. When I mentioned you and Pang, they showed great interest. Send me your resumés." I sent her my resumé with a note: "I'm only looking for one job. For myself." Hua hadn't known there was anything seriously wrong with my marriage.

Bringing up the issue of divorce with my family and with school officials would be difficult. The news would shock everyone because there had been no signs of strain between us. I hated to talk to the party secretary about my private life, but I needed an official letter from him granting me permission to apply for a divorce. But rumours travelled fast, and sooner than I expected I was summoned by Liu.

"What's going on?" he asked, nervously puffing a cigarette. There was no broad grin this time.

I pretended not to understand. "What do you mean?"

"I mean your divorce, of course. Everybody's talking about it. I want to know the truth."

"I want a divorce. What else can I tell you?"

After a long pause, Liu stood up and began pacing the room. "We haven't noticed any problems in your marriage. Did you have a fight? That's nothing. Every couple fights and then makes up."

"We're just not compatible."

"Think about it and we'll talk again, together with Pang," Liu said, looking very unhappy.

A week passed, and Liu seemed to have forgotten about our case. I couldn't afford to wait if I wanted to be in Beijing by the new year; it was already mid-November. I went to see him.

"If you want to talk about the same subject, bring Pang with you," he said. "I want to hear what he has to say."

On the way back to Liu's office later that day, I apologized to Pang: "I didn't want to drag you into this and embarrass you further, but I can't help it. Forgive me."

Once seated in Liu's office, Pang was stiff but not uneasy. He always had been able to stay cool even when he felt under attack. "The angrier I get, the more eloquent I become," he said.

"Now that I have you both here, I want to hear the whole story." Liu turned to Pang: "Do *you* really want the divorce?"

"Yes, it's by mutual agreement," Pang said. "And I don't want to have to explain anything, because it's a private matter."

Liu was dumbfounded. He had been expecting Pang to say he was opposed to the divorce. He muttered something about the wisdom of trying to weather the storm together, and dismissed us.

But he decided not to stand in our way, and I got the letters of permission I needed for both the transfer and the divorce. The transfer came with a condition: I had to find a job in Beijing within six months or return to Harbin. At least I was getting that much of a chance to make a break for freedom.

Getting the divorce papers could take a year. I wanted to get everything over with as quickly as possible; the longer we stayed together after deciding to separate, the more likely that anger and frustration would build.

Rumours about our separation were making the rounds. The authorities suspected it was connected with Daniel, but they had no evidence. The gossip on the outside and grief on the inside were a double burden for Pang, and one day he blew up. A trivial argument led to a fight, our third in ten years of marriage.

"I've had it! I'm not going to let you get away that easily!" His face was an angry red as he struck me several times with his fists. He hit me so hard that I wasn't able to go to work the next day, and I made up a story about falling off a table while hanging a picture.

I was horrified, but not because of the pain. I was afraid that, in his rage, he would go to the authorities and tell them about Daniel. Then life would really become hell. But he didn't.

We didn't talk to each other for a couple of days. Then one

evening he came into my room. I was lying in bed, my breasts still hurting and sprained thumb still swollen.

"I didn't mean to hit you," he said sadly. "It's the first time I've struck you and it'll be the last time, too. You must understand how humiliated I feel. Let's try to be nicer to each other during the last period of our life together. Forgive me this time."

I felt guilty. Why was he the one asking for forgiveness, when I had caused all our real problems? I had made life miserable for him, and he had been trying hard to be good to me.

I asked a friend to help us speed up the divorce by using his connections. He had a friend in the municipal government who agreed to write a letter: "Owing to a job transfer, please expedite the divorce papers of the two comrades mentioned here." After I handed in the letter, we got the divorce within a month.

On the day of my departure, a few friends came over for a farewell meal. Pang pretended nothing much was happening as he busied himself in the kitchen, where we had a last brief conversation.

"I hope you'll find a job in Beijing soon," he said.

"I'll try." I remembered the apartment keys in my pocket and gave them to him.

"You're handing over your power," he said, and tried to smile. I didn't know what to say. "If you ever need anything, write to me," he said gently. "Half of everything I have will always be yours. And if worst comes to worst, you can always come back to me." He was killing me with kindness. I bit my lip and hurried out of the kitchen, fighting tears. I'm really sorry, Pang, I thought. It's unfair to you, but I have to go.

The train was about to leave. On the platform stood my lover, my now-former husband and many dear friends. Suddenly I couldn't hold my head up any more; I couldn't face the scene. Here was one man who loved me; here was another who loved me just as much, and was sacrificing himself for me. I lowered my head and gave in to the sobs that had been building for months. As the train pulled out of the station and away from the waving hands, Lulu and I held each other, both weeping now. She waved to her adored father long after he was out of sight.

In Beijing, Lulu and I squeezed into my parents' two rooms, which already held my mother and father, Hua and her three grown children. There was no room for much furniture other than beds. My mother, Lulu and I shared a double bed; the others slept on cots.

My mother thought I was just visiting, as usual, for the winter vacation. Hua, who had suspected something was wrong with my marriage, said nothing. She didn't want to upset our mother with the prospect of another divorce in the family. My parents' four daughters and one son now had seven divorces between them: Hua, Wen and I had all divorced twice, and my brother Shen was in his second marriage. My eldest sister, Mei, was the exception: she married once and had five children.

The divorce rate in China is lower than in the West, but perhaps not as low as people are led to believe. In any case, the divorce rate in my family was certainly higher than the norm. Hua and I talked about this when I told her my marriage had ended.

"I think one reason for all the divorces is that our parents weren't exactly a loving couple," I said, "and so we carried no images in our heads of what a caring marriage might be like. Ma has always been so annoyed at everything her husband does or says; maybe her children have emulated that disgruntlement. And neither of them ever gave us much parental advice or guidance."

"I think history also has something to do with it; we were caught in the middle," Hua said. "By the time we reached marrying age, Pa was out of work, and boys from well-to-do families didn't want to marry into a family on the decline. But those were the kind of men we wanted as husbands.

"Then, after Liberation, men with family backgrounds similar to ours wanted to improve their chances by marrying into a worker or peasant family. So again, we were out of luck. But we never felt quite right marrying less educated, less sophisticated men. Our expectations outstripped what was available to us, and we never really felt satisfied."

I had high hopes about the vacancy at Hua's school. Soon after my arrival in Beijing, I was called for an interview, which went well. My interviewers said they would have to wait until my file arrived from Harbin before giving me a final answer. "I'm sure there'll be no problem," they said. "It's just a formality."

After a month of silence from the school, I asked Hua to find out what had happened. I felt confident about getting the job, so her answer came as a blow.

"You'll have to find work somewhere else," she said. "Now they say you're not suitable. I didn't ask any more questions."

I was devastated, and nervous. I approached a few other places, only to be told nothing was available. The months slipped by, and winter turned to spring. I was still being paid by Heida but if, after six months, I had no job, I also would have no salary, no Beijing resident permit and no ration coupons for grain. The permit and the coupons went with the job. With a child to feed, I was starting to worry. Had I made an awful mistake?

One day, shortly after the disappointing news from Hua's work unit, I bumped into Ken on the street. I had first met him at a party in the 1950s, not long after my return from East Germany. He seemed to have inherited everything from his Swiss mother; you could hardly detect anything Chinese in his features. He spoke excellent English, played decent jazz piano and could jitterbug; that was about all I knew about him.

I told Ken I was desperate to find a job. He suggested I try *China Reconstructs*, the English-language magazine where he worked. Since I hadn't worked on a publication before, I hesitated. "Don't worry," he said. "You'll quickly become familiar with the work. Come to the office tomorrow and I'll go with you to the personnel department. If you're not sure whether you'd like the work, don't make any commitment."

Make no commitment! What an absurd thought. The next day, I went to *China ReconStructs*, located in the Foreign Languages Press building in weSt Beijing. Ken, as promised, accompanied me to the interview with three senior editors and a party official. I was asked to describe, in English, my educational and work background. I was nervous; a lot was at stake. But before long, I was asked when I could start.

"I could come next week if you like," I said, trying to sound nonchalant. If they knew how desperate I was, they might become suspicious. Two days later Ken called to tell me I could start working on probation while the personnel department inveSti- gated my background. That cursed file again!

My file was transferred from Hua's school to *China ReconStructs*. For some reason, my family background and whatever else was in the file didn't bother them. Quite a few people working for the various publications at the Foreign Languages Press were from non-proletarian families, had been educated abroad, or had "com- plicated social conneCtions." I had also come along at a time when the magazine was looking for qualified people. It was a combina- tion of good luck and excellent timing.

Marta leFt Harbin for Canada, taking Rosa, toward the end of 1979. Daniel, meanwhile, had decided to extend his contraCt for another year, and their son Josh, now nine, stayed with him.

Daniel and I wrote to each other often. He sent his letters to my mother's place in Big Sweet Water Well Alley; I wrote to him care of a mutual friend in Harbin. I knew if I sent letters direCtly to him at Heida, other people would read them before he ever did. I numbered my letters, to help keep track of them. As far as we knew, no concrete evidence of our relationship had yet fallen into the hands of the authorities. They could only guess.

In one of his early letters, Daniel wrote: "I think about how much you mean to me and what life will be like this time next year. Up to now we've been dealing with expeCtation and anticipation. The hour of realization is growing closer.

"I always get nervous when the time comes to carry out something I've planned, especially something of importance. The nervousness arises from concern that an unforeseen flaw will appear and upset the plan. There's a principle that's become popular in North America called Murphy's Law. Simply stated, it says that if there's a chance for something to go wrong, it will.

"The kind of life we will lead in the coming years will require determination and sacrifice, particularly with regard to my financial obligation to Marta. I know how you feel about this and am glad you will be there to lend your support."

Although I derived strength from Daniel's letters, I still felt guilty towards Pang and Marta. Daniel wrote: "As for guilt, stop feeling miserable about it. I know Marta bears you no ill will. Guilt is for those who have done something wrong. Have you done anything wrong? Unpleasant, perhaps; wrong, no!"

He said he was expecting his divorce papers in May 1980, and his certainty helped lessen my own anxiety. He seemed to me a paragon of truth and justice when he wrote: "If there are obstacles imposed by any officials, I am quite prepared to take my case to the Canadian embassy and the foreign press. Such tactics will undoubtedly be unpleasant, but my love for you is strong enough that I will undergo the necessary hardship of publicity to realize something that is our human right."

In a letter he wrote in late May, Daniel enclosed a telegram from Marta: "Signed papers today. Will receive papers end May or beginning June." He was sure everything was proceeding apace at Marta's end, and he told me not to worry.

He was even more optimistic in his next letter. He said he had received the first set of documents from Marta's lawyer, and had broken the news to Jin in the Foreign Affairs Office. He had also asked for permission to stay in China beyond the end of his contract if the divorce papers hadn't arrived by then.

He wrote: "I, of course, told Jin why I want to remain in China. So, after months of obscurity, you will once again be in the news on campus. Rumours have been rampant.

"Josh has been told and likes the idea of a Chinese step-mother and a brainy step-sister. I think our children are mature for their ages and may be more adaptable than we give them credit for. At first he said he didn't want another mother, but when I said I wanted another wife, his resistance changed to understanding. He understands now the difference between a mother for him and a wife for dad."

What a relief! The universe was unfolding as it should.

My job at *China Reconstructs* was going well. The senior editors were pleased with my work, and I was beginning to make friends in the office. After my month's probation was up, they decided to keep me on. At the beginning of August, I was told by the personnel department to go back to Harbin and pick up the final documents that would seal my job transfer. I left immediately; my instincts told me I should go at once before anyone had second thoughts.

By this time, everyone at Heida knew that Daniel was going to marry me. People reacted in different ways: some were overly friendly and others very distant. Some went out of their way to offer me advice along the lines of: "Foreigners have different moral standards. They fall in love quickly; they fall out of love just as quickly. I hope Daniel's not like that."

But I walked around campus with my head held high, feeling, at last, like a winner. I was staying at a friend's home, and Daniel and Zhen came by for dinner.

"A toast to you, Daniel, my brother-in-law," Zhen said, and they clinked glasses. I wasn't sure whether she meant it or whether she still had her doubts about Daniel. But I was optimistic. Zhen did not, however, show up at the station on the day of my departure. I was crestfallen; the chances of us seeing each other again were slim.

"She can't come," Didi, another friend, told me. "She didn't want to start a war at home." I knew what Didi meant and I was grateful that she had come. Zhen's husband was not the only one who thought I was setting a bad example for other wives.

The day I returned to work, I was summoned to the personnel department. The news had finally reached Beijing.

The woman in charge of personnel was furious. "Why didn't you tell us about the foreigner? He's still married, as far as we know."

"But he's getting a divorce. He's got the first set of documents and the final papers will arrive any day."

"What if his wife changes her mind?"

"She wouldn't have sent the first set of documents if she didn't want the divorce."

"Are you planning to leave with him soon?"

"No. He wants to work here for a couple more years. His life and career will always be linked with China. I'll be with him wherever he decides to be, in China or anywhere else."

As soon as I left for Harbin, the personnel department had somehow learned that I was involved with a foreigner. They immediately sent a telegram informing Heida that my job offer was withdrawn. But the university insisted the decision could not be reversed. Neither place wanted me and for the same reason: my relationship with Daniel. I would have lost the job at *China Reconstructs* had the news of our relationship arrived in Beijing any earlier. For once, bureaucratic delay had been a blessing.

Chapter Thirteen

LIKE YIN AND YANG

After his contract ended in Harbin, Daniel came to Beijing with Josh. He tried to get a job, and several schools were pleased with the demonstration classes he gave. But none offered him a contract. All jobs for foreigners had to get the nod from the central Foreign Affairs Bureau in Beijing, and hiring Daniel would have implied official sanction of our relationship.

It was a time of tremendous uncertainty. We were waiting for his final divorce papers to arrive so that we could marry. But Daniel was starting to worry that, even after we were married, he would not be able to find work in China and that we would have to go to Canada until the scandal of our relationship died down.

With this plan in mind, he packed up the crate of possessions he was entitled to send to Canada when his Heida contract ended. I bought some new clothes for myself and household goods for our future home, which we included in the shipment. This seemed sensible; it might be some time before Daniel could find work in Canada and money would be tight.

In this period of limbo, Daniel and Josh were camping at various Canadian friends' apartments. They came over every evening to my mother's place, where they stayed until after supper. Although we saw each other every day, Daniel and I had nowhere to be alone. One day he asked the friend they were staying with if he could invite me over for the afternoon. Andrew McLean, who worked for the Canadian embassy, didn't mind; and Josh could go and stay with my mother.

Although this was not the first diplomat's apartment I'd been in, I was still impressed: living-room, dining room, kitchen, bathroom, and two bedrooms with closets you could walk into! A freezer in the kitchen was packed with meat.

Daniel led me into the room where he slept. He suspected the rooms were bugged, but at this point we didn't care. At last we had a rare moment alone.

A week later I was invited to a party at the same apartment, where I met some of Andrew's diplomat friends. The next day, one of my colleagues let it drop that he knew where I had been the night before. But how did he know? From the taxi driver who took us there? The cook? A surveillance camera in the building or bugs in the apartment? I never found out.

A few weeks later, Daniel and Josh came to my mother's place for our usual Sunday stroll. On our way out, I heard Josh asking: "Shall we tell her now?"

"Later," Daniel said. He seemed unusually terse, and I had a sense of foreboding. We walked silently to the Forbidden City.

Once we were lost in the throng of people, he began: "I called Marta last night. She was furious, cursing and calling me names. She's changed her mind and said if I want a divorce, I'll have to go back and do the rest of the paperwork myself."

I was stunned. My legs felt weak. "What are you going to do?"

"I have to go back without you. There's no other way."

"When will you go?"

"In about two weeks."

I fell silent. Daniel had his camera with him and wanted Josh to take pictures of us. I turned my head away. No. Not now.

Daniel had wanted to break the news to me away from my home, so no one would be watching when I threw a fit. He didn't expect me to react so calmly. He was forgetting that even in times of extreme joy or sorrow, Chinese consider losing control a sign of weakness.

Little was said on the walk home. Only Daniel spoke: "Our relationship has gone too far now to back out. Don't worry. I'll come back. But I need some time. I'll never forgive myself if I don't take you with me."

I didn't know what to say. But my instincts told me that once he was gone it would not be easy for him to come back. The situation at home would be too complex and too emotional for him to walk away from.

Once back at my mother's place, I couldn't control myself any longer. I went into a room by myself, covered my face with a towel and sobbed bitterly. Daniel walked in and put his arms around me. "At last you've let it out. I was worried when you kept so silent." His voice and his touch only made me cry harder.

My mother heard us and came in from outside. "What's happened?" she asked.

"Nothing," I said. I couldn't bring myself to tell her.

The next two weeks were spent getting Daniel ready for his departure. My mother went out one afternoon and came back with a pair of black cotton shoes.

"Don't forget her," she said as she gave them to Daniel. "These shoes will help you walk faster. They'll bring you back sooner." Daniel was touched by the gesture. And I was struck by how unusual it was for a woman of my mother's generation to accept these events so gracefully.

Daniel needed a job offer to get a visa to return to China. New World Press, a division of the Foreign Languages Press, said they would keep a job open for him. He assured them he would return in five months.

On his last day in Beijing, we both avoided talking about the one subject that concerned us most. At one point, he took off his grandfather's ring, which was also his wedding band. He slipped it on my finger and said: "Keep this for me. I'll come back and get it." With this ring on my finger, I felt there was some hope that he would.

"I will come back," he whispered, after kissing me goodbye at the airport. My eyes followed him as he moved slowly out of sight. He didn't turn around.

During his stop-over in Vancouver, he mailed a letter saying how much he missed me and hoped we would be together soon. Another letter, sent from Toronto, said he could begin to plan a course of action once he had talked with Marta. But after he arrived back in his home town, I didn't hear from him. Every day I raced home from work hoping to find mail, but every day only disappointment awaited me. Nothing came in the first month, nor the second. My anxiety grew as time went by.

My family members looked worried, but no one wanted to raise the subject. Ken would take me out for long walks and gently urge me to talk. He was afraid I would get sick if I kept everything bottled up: "Get angry, yell, cry, but just don't keep silent." If it hadn't been for Ken, I might have gone crazy. I was heartbroken.

Eventually I wrote to Daniel, care of his brother in Toronto, asking for an explanation for the long silence. Three weeks later I received a reply. It was written on January 5, 1981, two months and 20 days after his departure. It began: "I'm very sorry for not having written sooner, but I have not found it easy to sit down at the typewriter. First, let me say that I have failed. Yes, it's true. That's something I never thought I would have to say." I couldn't go on reading. The paper fell from my hand.

Hua picked up the letter: "Is it from him?" I nodded and she didn't ask a second question. Everything was written on my face.

Daniel wrote that he was living with Marta again because of the children and for financial reasons. But, he said, he felt torn between two women and two countries: "I feel imprisoned here. I miss you and China so much. I keep thinking about that wonderful job offered by New World Press. I see myself walking through the wintry streets of Beijing with you at my side. I am a foreigner here, thinking of my home across the sea. News about China is eagerly devoured. Never have I felt so frustrated.

"Then I look at Marta, Josh and Rosa and see how happy they are here. How could such a thing happen? Both of us are unlucky; it's just that my misfortune came later than yours. What about your life? What makes it bearable? Now that I've handed you another disappointment, can we still go on dreaming?"

I wrote back sounding miserable. I wanted him to understand what a difficult position he had put me in.

His second letter arrived in February: "I remember the first time I saw you, back in 1977 when I was teaching the first class at Heida. You sat at the back furiously taking notes, obviously understanding everything I said. Even then, I felt a bond between us. Here were two people who were destined to share something together. We will fulfill this destiny. I know it.

"Having to leave you behind to face so many unknown forces alone has torn my heart. My conscience will not let me rest until I have you at my side again. Neither of us can be whole until this is done. Being a half-person is unbearable."

His romantic declarations didn't move me as they once had. I no longer trusted him. I went to visit Andrew and told him about Daniel's latest letter, and my doubts.

"I know it's hard for you to get over this," Andrew said, "but just try to store it somewhere at the back of your head. We all have some unpleasant experience like this at some time in our lives." He paused. "Is there anything I can do for you?"

"I want to go abroad to study, but I don't want any help from Daniel. It's hard for me now to face my family, friends, colleagues. What will my future be like here? I'll carry a dossier stained with disgrace all my life."

Andrew said he didn't have many connections with universities. "But send me your resumé and I'll see what I can do." He seemed so sincere, and I felt that he was the only person who might be able to help.

A few weeks later I received another letter from Canada, this time from Greg, an old friend of Daniel's whom I had met several times. He wrote: "Danny says he wants a divorce, but he's not prepared just to walk out on Marta. And he wants the kids. So, he must leave Marta with a good job and good prospects. But how long will that take? It's counted in years, not months. It takes years to find a position where you really belong back in Canada after having cut ties.

"I turned the conversation to you, Zhimei, to find out what he felt. I talked about the risks you had taken and the commitment you had made for him. But the conversation fell dead. I turned the conversation to admiration of your strength and determination. Danny echoed this. I said I didn't know whether he realized what you had gone through. He realized. He also knew that Marta did not really want the divorce. But as soon as he could, he would divorce her, even though you, Zhimei, might not still be around to marry him.

"At one point, Danny said flippantly: 'You know, I could be perfectly happy married to two women. Of course, it would be pretty hard to get either of them to go along with it . . . Why don't you marry Zhimei, Greg?'

"What more can I say, Zhimei? As time goes by, you must recede. Even now, you are not so important that Danny is prepared to give up everything for you. But I do not believe your life will be shattered by this. This is not worthy of shattering you."

No one in my family said or asked anything about Daniel, but I moved out of my mother's place; I needed solitude. I couldn't go on pretending life was normal. I knew the neighbours were gossiping after having seen Daniel at our place, after having heard Josh call me Ma and my mother Grandma. None of this could be wiped out by pretending it had never happened.

I put a cot in the corner of the *China Reconstructs* office, next to my typewriter. In the evening, after colleagues had gone home, I was left alone, surrounded by typewriters and scattered books and papers. What was there in life to keep me going?

Work.

Yes, work would help me forget. I selected a powerful story, "Spring within Winter," written by a woman about her determination to overcome the hardships of working on a state farm in the harsh northeast and of her longing for love. I began translating it into English to keep myself busy.

When my colleagues arrived back in the morning, no matter how miserable I had been feeling overnight, I kept up a cheerful front. I was determined to maintain my pride and dignity, from which, someday, I would derive the strength to get back on my feet. But I was confused, and haunted by unanswered questions: Had we both been blinded by love? Or had I just been used to ease the tension in Daniel's marriage?

I felt guilty about having insisted Lulu come with me to Beijing. She was miserable when we first arrived; every night, she buried her head in the quilt and wept. I tried to comfort her, but she didn't want me to touch her. It was torture to lie awake listening to her sobs. How could I do this to her? Whenever anyone said anything negative about Harbin, she would jump to its defence. I knew she was defending her father, not Harbin.

After I moved into the office, I went back to my mother's on weekends. Lulu would phone me at work and ask when I was coming back, and I could hear her sniffles at the other end of the line. Her artistic ability became apparent in that period: she drew when she felt lonely, using the backs of old calendars to draw figures dressed in traditional Chinese costumes.

Two months later I was given a small room in a dormitory at the back of the office. There was no kitchen; everybody cooked in the corridor. There was only one toilet for the dozen families living on the same floor. But I was happy with the arrangement; I had my own home again. I moved in a bed from my mother's, and borrowed a table and a bookshelf from the office. The things I had bought to start a new life had been shipped to Canada in Daniel's crate, and I had no savings left to buy anything new.

I tried to sound cheerful when Lulu came to visit the week after I moved in. "Isn't it neat and tidy here? And there's more space to move around than at Grandma's place."

Lulu drank tea out of a tin thermos lid, because I only had one mug. She asked if we could go out to dinner, but I didn't have the money. A few days later, she came to my office. "Auntie Kang came from Harbin and gave me twenty yuan from Dad. Here, you have it." I took her in my arms, not knowing what to say. She was only eleven, but seemed to understand my troubles. We spent more than ten yuan in a restaurant that night; more than we could afford, but Lulu was happy, and so was I.

After a year-and-a-half of silence, Daniel wrote again, in March 1983, saying he now had a job that would bring him to China several times in the next year to set up a language program in Hunan province.

"It would seem there is no end to the grief I have caused you. My conscience will give me no rest to the end of my days," he wrote. "The shoes your mother gave me will do what she intended them to do, but not under the circumstances we all wished for in 1980. Two-and-a-half years is not a long time in terms of healing the wounded heart and soul. We have each borne our burdens in our separate ways."

A few weeks later, he phoned my office from Beijing. He said he had brought some of my things back and we arranged to meet at my office that evening. After I put down the phone, I started to cry. Hearing his voice so close, I realized the love, no matter how injured, was still there. I had mixed feelings: I wanted to see him again, but was scared of touching the raw wound.

That evening, we greeted each other with a handshake and sat stiffly side by side in two armchairs, both looking straight ahead.

Daniel broke the ice. "I've brought some of your things back and I'll bring the rest next time."

Silence.

"Say something," he said. "Curse me, say you hate me, just say something."

I was trying so hard to control myself that I was trembling. I took a deep breath and began: "You once said we were both selfish people. You can say that about yourself, but not about me. You want everything, but you're not prepared to make any sacrifices. I've given up nearly everything, and you've given up absolutely nothing."

Daniel lit his pipe and starting puffing. "Yes, it is unfair. I was wrong. Can you forgive me?"

Another long silence. I wasn't ready to say that I forgave him everything. And I was fighting tears. "I think you'd better go. It's getting late."

I stood at the entrance to the building, watching as he moved away with his long strides. I was dazed. Our meeting after so long apart had felt awkward, unreal.

That autumn he reappeared, bringing more of my things. Again we met, again our conversation was stiff. But this time his expression told me he had more to say, although perhaps was scared to say it. A letter was waiting for me when I got home that evening. I recognized his handwriting at once.

"It's been a long time since I last wrote. Don't think that it's because I haven't thought of you; I have, every single day since 1980. This letter is written with some reservations, since I dread the thought of doing anything to cause you any more pain.

"My dilemma was loving two women and not finding a way to make both happy. Of the two, I knew you were stronger. Knowing what you have experienced and survived in your life convinced me to choose the way I did. Your strength, dignity, pride and determination made you truly beautiful in my eyes.

"When I left you in 1980, standing in the Beijing airport, alone with your sadness and my grandfather's ring, I think we both knew, but were loath to admit, that our lives were not going to be spent together. Like yin and yang, we were fated to co-exist and will continue to do so. In a way I have given birth to you and you to me. I feel we have known each other before in a far and long-forgotten time. We have been one and that will never change. As we go our separate ways, there will always be a delicate thread linking us. The legacy of our unhappy love is that wherever you are, I will be with you."

As I read the letter, our past together flooded back. I thought he was no longer in my heart, but it wasn't true. On the envelope, he had written the time of his planned departure from Beijing. I hardly slept that night, struggling with whether to call him. In the morning, I called.

"Were you drunk when you wrote the letter?" I asked.

"A little. I wrote it right after a banquet. But when I delivered it to your place, I was completely sober." I almost wished he had said he was drunk. That would have made things easier for me.

"I'll be coming back in February. Write me if there's anything I can do for you in Canada," Daniel added.

I felt torn. Should I forgive him and give him a chance to remedy what he'd done? Or should I leave well enough alone and let him live with his guilty conscience?

When Daniel returned in February 1984, I took him to my mother's place. She was delighted to see him wearing the cotton shoes she had given him three years earlier. But she didn't know that he had not come back to get me. I couldn't bear to tell her; she had had so many shattered dreams.

Daniel took her to lunch at the Jianguo, a luxury hotel built in partnership with a Hong Kong firm. Her excitement lasted a whole week as she stood in her courtyard telling envious neighbours about everything she had seen.

Daniel was back in my life, forgiven. It was hard for some people to understand why, especially Ken, who had helped me through my earlier miseries. But despite all the hurt Daniel had caused me, I still couldn't resist his appeal. The feeling of oneness was still there. We both thought it might be possible to resume a relationship, albeit with lowered expectations. I knew now that we would never be husband and wife.

Soon after he left again for Canada, I received a letter from him: "You have taught me the beauty of forgiveness, the power of dignity and value of friendship. Though I have erred greatly in my treatment of you and suffered deeply for it, I make this new beginning with hope and some fear, for as I once again leave you here in this often hostile environment, I constantly feel concern for your safety and tenuous personal freedom.

"The one thing you and I want most cannot be given now. I can't say if it can ever be given, but there is still the small flame of hope within me. Without that I would never have come back into your life and exposed you to a reawakening of what had been long asleep." He ended the letter with the circular symbol of yin and yang, the male and female principles at the heart of Chinese philosophy. Beside it he wrote: "We are one."

Chapter Fourteen

THE WHITE BOBBYPIN GANG

Daniel returned in the summer of 1984, on his way to take up residence in Hunan. His family would follow a few months later. The day before he left, we went on an outing to the Fragrant Hills in Beijing's western suburbs. We joined the long line for the cable-car and during the wait, stood close together, chatting and laughing. When our turn came, we jumped into the cable-car; it jerked as it passed joints on the cable, and Daniel put a reassuring arm around me. At the top, we looked for a quiet place to spend the afternoon. On a secluded hilltop, I spread out a towel for us to sit on.

Once we were settled, Daniel put an arm around me and we kissed. "So nice to have a bit of peace and quiet," he said.

Suddenly, two men jumped out from a bush behind us, brandishing ID cards. "We're security!" said the younger one, whom we later nicknamed Baby-face. "And we've seen everything."

"They must be interrogated separately," said the older man, whom we nicknamed Big Brother. Daniel and I scrambled to our feet and Big Brother led me aside. I felt faint and held on to some rocks. My head was buzzing.

"I'll need your name, age, marital status, work unit and nature of your relationship with the foreigner. How do you know him? When and where did you meet?" And on and on. I answered honestly, but Big Brother wasn't satisfied.

"You understand that by kissing in public you're scandalizing public morals? What were you planning to do here?"

"Nothing."

"That's a lie! We'll treat you leniently if you're honest. Look, I'm a married man. You don't have to be shy with me."

"We didn't do anything."

"If we hadn't shown up, you two would have gone much further than kissing. That's why you brought that big towel. You're a divorced woman. You have no man at home now. Look, I know how that feels. I understand."

I stared at him in disgust, thinking: "Dirty old man! You're getting a kick out of this. If I had wanted to sleep with this man, I wouldn't have come here." But I thought it best to remain silent, which annoyed him. He was after a lurid confession.

"Well," he said, "it's up to you whether you say anything or not. But your attitude isn't good, and you'll have to come with us to the security bureau. We'll need to put this on record."

Out of the corner of my eye I could see that Baby-face seemed to be having a pleasant chat with Daniel. Foreigners and Chinese get different treatment every time! Daniel was amusing him by imitating a Hunan accent.

"I told them that kissing a good friend is perfectly normal in our culture," he told me later. The security men decided Daniel could leave, but that I had to stay.

"No way," Daniel said. "We came together and we're leaving together." Big Brother told me to explain to Daniel that China's regulations were meant to govern its own citizens. But Daniel insisted on coming with me.

Baby-face took me aside and whispered: "We didn't want to embarrass you, but, you know, we have a quota every month and if we don't meet it, we lose our bonus." I looked at him in amazement, despising and pitying him at the same time. Was he trying to make a deal?

"If you want money, I'll give you some," I said.

"No, no," he said. "That's not what I meant."

How dumb! Why did I ask? Why didn't I just stuff some money in his hands?

Quotas, quotas for everything. The police detain people on the basis of insufficient evidence, because there's a quota. Trees are planted on dry, rocky slopes where they haven't a chance of growing, because there's a quota. Workers finish their assigned tasks in a week and idle away the rest of the month with no qualms, because they've fulfilled their quota.

As we were walking to the cable-car, I caught sight of a man in sunglasses. We had seen him earlier as we made our way up the hill. Now he was grinning, perhaps in victory. Had he alerted the police? At the cable-car, the ticket collector said to our guards: "I see you've made a catch today!" My face was burning.

At the security bureau, I was questioned by two men in uniform as Daniel waited outside. "You must write a confession. But first you must admit that you've violated Article 4 of our regulations." He pointed to a poster on the wall listing the "safety rules" for the mountain area. I didn't want to be detained for hours and keep Daniel waiting, so I did as I was told and signed my name beside my fingerprint.

"You mustn't tell the foreigner anything about what has happened in this room," one of the police said. "This is the rule."

As Big Brother led me out of the compound, his tone changed: "Don't worry. We won't report this to your work unit. But be careful next time. Choose a more discreet place."

The next day, I was called in for questioning by the personnel department of my work unit. Big Brother had lied: he had reported everything, adding one more black mark to my record.

My encounters with the police were only beginning. Not long after the Fragrant Hills episode, I received a troubling phone call from the police station near my home. They wanted to question Lulu, who was now living with me: "No matter how late she gets in, bring her to the station tonight."

"What is it? Why so urgent?" I thought the mother of a teenager had the right to know.

"We can't tell you," the caller said, and hung up.

I went out to the bus stop every half hour, straining to catch sight of Lulu. On my fourth trip, around 8:00 p.m., she did get off a bus, looking as cheerful as ever. We walked up the stairs in silence. Once inside our room, I said gently: "Tell me, Lulu. Have you done anything wrong?"

"No."

"Then why do the police want to see you?"

"Oh, I know," she said nonchalantly. "They want to ask about the hand-copied book. They've already asked some of my friends."

"Hand-copied book?" I was alarmed when I saw her blush.

"I didn't read it, honest! I . . . I only had a quick look. I couldn't understand what was in it, anyway."

I realized what she was talking about. Pulp romances had started to appear in Beijing. They were hardly sexually explicit; in them, couples embraced and kissed. But even these were thought to be "corrupting the morals of young people," and it was well known that the police were searching for the source of the books.

"All right, if that's all it is, don't worry. We'd better go and clear this up. Just tell them what you know and don't make anything up."

At the police station, Lulu was led away for questioning.

"Do you know what they want my daughter for?" I asked an officer.

"They want to check something with her," he said absentmindedly, then changed the subject: "What does your husband do?"

"I'm by myself." There was such stigma attached to the word divorced that I always tried to avoid it; women were only divorced because they were "bad."

After a while, he told me to go and wait for Lulu at home: "This could take some time."

When Lulu wasn't home by midnight, I woke Yan, who was

visiting from Anhui. We set off for the police station and soon saw three figures approaching: two policemen escorting Lulu home.

"Take Pang Lu home," one of the officers said to Yan and, turning to me: "We need to talk to you alone."

After Lulu and Yan left, the officer said Lulu had told them what she knew about the hand-written book making the rounds at school. But now they wanted to know more about her relationship with a certain boy.

"We've tried to make her understand she won't be blamed for anything she's done," he said, "because we'll view her as the victim. But we can't get anything out of her. We trust you'll co-operate."

When I got home, Lulu was at her desk as usual, doing her homework. I couldn't believe that my fourteen-year-old was taking all this so staunchly, more so than myself.

Lulu was summoned to the station again the next day. When I got there after work, I caught sight of her through the small window of an interrogation room. I beckoned to a policeman, who came out into the hall.

"What's going on?" I asked. "She's been here for hours."

"This daughter of yours is really stubborn. We can't make her say a thing," he said.

"She may be stubborn, but she doesn't make things up," I said. "What are you trying to get out of her?"

"She's been seen with boys," he said.

"Yes? Doing what?"

"Skating, going for walks, seeing movies."

"What's wrong with that?"

"Well, there's more. From what we've learned, we think she may have had improper relations with a boy."

I didn't want euphemisms and vague explanations, I wanted the facts: "How do you know?"

"We analyzed the situation."

I was angry now. "What does that mean? Facts must be proven, not just 'analyzed.' I'm taking her home. And I want the investigation brought to some sort of conclusion. The case can't just remain open like this."

"Now look," he said, "what we're doing is confidential. We don't even tell each other exactly how we're proceeding with a case. So I can't give you a 'conclusion.' Maybe we'll need to interview her again, maybe not."

It was eerie. History seemed to be repeating itself. At a criticism session during the Cultural Revolution, it came out that I "hung around with hooligans as a teenager. It's recorded in your file." The "hooligans" were my sister's classmates, who we went ballroom dancing with. It really was a vicious circle.

After her unpleasant run-in with the police, I tried to spend more time with Lulu. I was worried about how it might have affected her. One evening while we were watching television, she said quietly: "Ma, can you get me out of the country? I don't want to stay here. I'm treated differently at school now."

Her words drove into my heart like sharp needles. My voice shook as I struggled to reply: "I would if I could, Lulu." We just looked at each other, with eyes that said: what a life!

Lulu started to dislike school; teachers were criticizing her now more than ever. But changing schools was not easy. You needed permission from the one school to leave and from the other to enrol. We did find a school that was willing to take her, until, that is, they received an anonymous letter. A friend of mine worked at the school, saw the letter and told me of its contents. It said Lulu was "a bad girl, with a history of violence," and that the police had interrogated her as a suspected member of the White Bobbypin Gang.

I was shocked. What on earth was the White Bobbypin Gang? I never did find out what they meant. Surely the school wouldn't accept this anonymous rubbish as fact?

"Also," my friend added, "there's a paragraph that says nasty things about her mother." He regretted telling me that when he saw me blanch. I considered asking my friend to get me a copy of the letter, but what could I have done with it? No one would have helped me trace the handwriting.

Lulu had to stay at her old school and face endless humiliation from the teachers. She was labelled an "undisciplined student" and the following evidence recorded in her file:

She doesn't mix with the good students in class (read: the goody-goodies who try to curry favour with the teachers).

She came to school in jeans after a teacher warned her she would cut the legs off if she wore them again.

She hit a classmate (to stop her bullying another girl).

She talks casually with boys.

She persists in wearing a white bobbypin that a teacher has told her is only worn by bad elements.

In April 1982 I got a letter of admission and a scholarship offer from the journalism school of the University of King's College in Halifax, Nova Scotia. Only later did I realize what a miracle this was. At the time, I had no idea how difficult it was to get a scholarship as a foreign student in Canada.

I asked my boss for permission to leave, but the answer was no. He said I should have asked for permission before applying to the school, not after. So I went over his head to the top officials at my work unit, visiting each of the three in turn. I finally got permission from them to apply for a passport. But when I took my application to the Public Security Bureau, I was told that even though I had a scholarship, I would need a sponsor.

My heart sank. I had no relatives in the West. The only people I could approach were the foreigners I had become friendly with in the past few years. One of them readily agreed to sign an affidavit of support, which I presented to the security bureau.

"This is not a relative," I was told.

I started to suspect that my work unit was obstructing my application after all. One of my colleagues who had connections in the security bureau confirmed my suspicion. He found out I was on a list the police kept of "people with problems" who they were supposed to keep an eye on. And, barring a change in policy, no one on the list would ever be allowed to leave the country.

At about this time it was also announced that people over forty-five would not be allowed to study abroad. I was already two years over the limit. The door was now firmly shut. But the more impossible my chances appeared, the harder I pursued the goal.

I could tell I was being followed whenever I met any of my foreign friends. The risks I ran in order to keep in touch with them were more than compensated for by their warmth, and moral support. The friendships with people from different cultures had enriched my life. For me, there was also an element of escapism; the time spent with foreigners felt like a respite from all the tension in my life. But what if the security police tired of this cat-and-mouse game and just packed me off to a remote area to be lost in oblivion? It had happened to others, and I lived in fear of the same fate.

I had arranged to meet Andrew one afternoon in front of the Friendship Store. As usual, I was early and he was late. As I was watching out for his black Mercedes, I suddenly noticed three men approaching me on bicycles. In dark sunglasses, they looked every bit the part of security police. They formed a menacing semicircle around me, saying nothing. I felt weak. Heart pounding, I began to move away. It was not the first time I had been followed, but it was the first time they had come up and stood right beside me. I made it as far as a traffic-police booth by the side of the road and tried to grab hold of a lamppost by the curb. Then I blacked out.

When I came to, I was no longer on the sidewalk. I was now right in front of the Friendship Store, about ten metres away from where I had collapsed, and surrounded by strange faces.

I was still dizzy and very confused. My pants were torn, my arms and hands were bruised, my mouth was bleeding and my blouse was stained with blood. I heard a woman say: "Someone should take her to the hospital!" Then a man: "Who's going to take *her*!?"

As I tried to stand up, an older woman reached out to help me.

A man appeared and offered to drive me to hospital. I looked up and saw that he was in uniform.

"Thanks, but I'm OK. I'll just go home now." His uniform made me nervous.

"Ma!" said a voice in the crowd. I couldn't believe my ears. It was Yan. She looked horrified. "What on earth happened to you?"

"I don't know. I felt sick," I whispered. "What are you doing here?" She and her boyfriend had managed to get entry passes for the Friendship Store, normally reserved for foreigners. They had seen the crowd as they left the store.

At that moment, Andrew appeared. "What happened?" he asked, looking in astonishment at my dishevelled state. "Are you all right? Can you walk? Let me take you home."

As I got into his car, I noticed a policeman going into his booth and picking up a phone. They were going to keep track of the car.

"Tell me what happened," Andrew said. "Did someone hit you?"

"I don't know. I blacked out. I don't know what happened after that."

"But your face and lips are swollen, and your clothes are torn. How did this happen?"

"I can't explain it, Andrew." I touched my mouth and discovered that one of my front teeth had been pushed up into my gums. "God, I'm so nervous."

"What you need, Zhimei, is a bath and a brandy," Andrew said, and he swung his car into a side-street. He drove around until he felt sure we had no police escort.

At Andrew's place, after a hot bath, I put on some of his clothes and threw my torn and bloodied ones away. I was still in shock and terrified. The whole episode was probably meant to have that effect, to feed my growing paranoia.

I was afraid to talk, imagining I saw listening devices wherever I looked. I scribbled on a piece of paper: "Can you help me? It's not just for me but for my children's sake." Andrew read the note, and said nothing as he tore it into small pieces.

"Look, Zhimei," he said while driving me home, "you know I'd like to help. But what can I do? I can't hide you at the embassy. I can't marry you. In the diplomatic service, we're not allowed to marry nationals of a communist country."

"I understand your situation, Andrew. I don't want to do anything illegal or get you into any trouble. It's just that I'm desperate now."

For a week I didn't go to work. I had my tooth fixed, saw a doctor and stayed home, nursing mental and physical bruises. My colleagues thought I had developed some sort of heart trouble because of the tension of recent months. Ken was the only person at work who knew the truth, and he worried about my safety.

Having failed in my attempts to get a passport, I decided to try another route. Shenzhen, the special economic zone near Hong Kong, was looking for professionals and had set up a recruiting office in Beijing. My interview went splendidly until I was asked my age. As soon as I replied, the interview was over. The age limit for recruits was forty-five.

When all roads out of China seemed closed to me, my father suffered a stroke. He was partially paralysed and lost the ability to speak. After several weeks in hospital, we took him home to my mother, and there seemed to be immediate improvement in his condition.

When he gestured that he wanted to sit up in bed, we propped him up with two plump pillows. Then he pointed to a book he wanted placed in his hands: an English grammar that for years had been the only book he read. He used to sit for hours holding that book, sometimes reading it, sometimes not. It seemed to be his form of meditation, or, in my mother's view, of escape.

In the past, she had been tempted many times to throw the book away. "He's pretending to read it," she would mutter. "He just doesn't want to help with the housework." In fact, my father used to do a lot of the housework and most of the cooking. My mother was just being faithful to a pattern established early in their married life. She had grown used to complaining about him.

My father had been home for only one week, propped up in bed, smiling at his favourite book, when he died. Over time, my youthful impatience with what I saw as his meekness and passivity had turned to awareness of the humiliation he was made to suffer in the second half of his life, and sympathy for the anguish he felt at not being able to support his family. "I was born with nothing and I shall leave this world with nothing," he used to say, and he was right.

Although their life together had never been peaceful, my mother was lonely without him. Her own health began to decline after his death. In China, many believe that when an old person dies, their partner will soon follow.

One morning in November 1984, a month after my father's death, a colleague burst into my office waving a postcard. "Zhimei, look what I've got here! A notice from the Public Security Bureau. You're going to get your passport!"

I couldn't believe my ears. I had been trying to get a passport for three years and was losing hope. "You're kidding?"

"I'm serious. I found it on the windowsill in the doorman's room. It might easily have been lost if I hadn't noticed it."

There was just one sentence on the postcard: "Do you still want to go to Canada?"

I had heard rumours of a relaxation in the policy governing people wanting to go abroad, but by now I wasn't pinning my hopes on anything. I wrote at once to the Public Security Bureau confirming that I wanted to leave, and took the note there myself to ensure delivery. A week later they notified me. I went back to the security bureau, filled in another form, paid fifteen yuan and was given a passport. It had suddenly become so matter-of-fact.

I walked slowly to the bus stop, staring at the little brown booklet. It was hard to believe it was real.

When I told my boss I had finally been issued a passport, he said: "But what use is it now? Your scholarship offer is long gone." He preferred to see misfortune befall me than celebrate any ray of hope.

I cabled Andrew, who had recently been transferred back to Ottawa: "Passport obtained." A few days later, he called and asked why I thought it had finally happened.

"I guess because everybody else is getting a passport, too," I said. "But now I don't have a school to go to."

"Write to King's College. I'll give them a call, too. And don't worry about your plane ticket. I'll send you one." Andrew was always willing to help, expecting nothing in return.

I wrote to King's College, which by now had a new director. George Bain had accepted me two years earlier, but, to my surprise, Walter Stewart wrote back immediately readmitting me. He also raised the amount of monthly bursary promised me, to take into account the inflation in the two years since I was first accepted. It all seemed so unbelievable.

In February 1985, two months before I left China, Daniel came to Beijing on business. We hadn't seen each other since the summer, when we were questioned because of a kiss. He came to my home one afternoon. I made a pot of tea, and we sat side by side on the couch.

"Marta is upset all over again," he said. "I can't hide things from her anymore. She knows we saw each other again last summer."

I had been half expecting an announcement like this. There was a long silence as I poured our tea and weighed my words. "It's time we stopped seeing each other completely, Daniel."

He lit his pipe as he pondered his reply. Finally, he spoke: "Other men have lovers because they don't love their wives. But this is not my case. I love my wife."

I felt estranged from him, and awkward in his presence. Once again, a chasm had opened between us.

"The heart can be broken once, but not twice," I said. "It's best if we go our separate ways. I'd rather you didn't look for me in Canada."

Daniel sat silently, staring at his pipe.

"You're doing fine again, Daniel. You've re-established your reputation in China. And there's a lot more you can do here. Be happy with what you have."

"But with you gone, half the attraction of China is gone," he said, turning towards me. I got up and went over to the window, and he knew I wanted him to leave.

"We kept a distance like this when I first returned to China. Now we're separating in the same way," he said sadly.

"It's better this way." I didn't look around, and we separated without even a handshake. I stood at the window and watched him go. I knew I would never feel the same about another man. The illusions, the passion, the pain, the hopes and disappointment would never be as intense as they were with Daniel.

Before leaving Beijing the next day, he mailed a letter, the last he would write to me: "Our last meeting yesterday was hard for me and, in spite of what you may say, hard I think for you, too. I don't think I've ever loved you more than I did yesterday. The past is ever with us. The future is partly yours, partly fate's; to what degree of each I cannot say. If you do succeed in forgetting all, my memories are sufficient for two.

"Be well, be happy, be safe and believe that if you really need, and all else fails, I will respond. I doubt it will be necessary. So many people are pulling for you. Have you ever determined why so many and why so much? You are special and we all know it.

"The roar of reality drowns out the cry of desire. That's our karma. Your star is now in the ascent. It will give me great pleasure to watch it rise."

Getting ready to leave was emotional because I knew I would not be coming back soon. There were so many arrangements to make and goodbyes to say. Pang came down to Beijing to collect Lulu; he would take care of her after I left.

Leaving my mother was difficult. The day of my departure in April 1985 was our last together. She died eight months later and was buried beside my father.

Despite the importance Chinese families place on sons, I had always been my mother's favourite. She pinned her hopes on me; through me she sought to live vicariously the life of a strong and independent woman that had been denied to her. It was a shock when I learned of her death. I thought she would live long enough to take pleasure in all the achievements of my new life. And I had wanted so much to bring her to Canada to share my happiness in her few remaining years.

As we were parting, she said something she had often said in times of difficulty: "Don't be afraid, Zhimei, even if the walls are caving in around you."

Another thing she used to say was: "If today you make me a queen, I'll live like a queen. But if tomorrow you make me a beggar, I'll also survive." Indeed, when circumstances changed, she quickly took up the challenge and underwent a remarkable transformation. In my youth, she had been a mahjong addict who had little time for anyone else. But when it fell to her to support the family, she overcame her addiction, started a small business, raised chickens, treadled on a sewing machine all day, took up knitting. She tried everything she could think of to put food on the table and, without her, the family would have collapsed.

I always thought of her as a special, unusual woman who, with her optimism, self-confidence and determination, set an example for me to follow. Women of her generation had bound or liberated feet, but she also had a liberated mind, full of ideas that were ahead of her time. I had enormous respect for her and disliked her only when she made my father feel inadequate.

I asked for permission to resign from my work unit, which should have entitled me to severance pay calculated on the basis of the thirty-four years I had worked in the People's Republic. I wanted to be able to give the money to my daughters. I received permission to resign, but not the right to claim the money. Right to the end, the personnel department seemed determined to make things difficult for me. But I had neither the time nor the energy to fight this round with them.

"Look at it this way," Ken said. "It's just one more price you have to pay for your freedom."

The departure was wrenching: I was giving up everything I had built over the years. I was leaving family and friends, and exchanging a familiar culture for one of unknowns and uncertainties. I would have to find my own way, alone, out there in a world of competition, which many people believed was a man's world. I would have to build a new life at the age of fifty, when many people thought there was no point trying.

I left Beijing with mixed feelings: fear of the future combined with determination to leave a society that would never fully accept me. I had faced discrimination in my own culture and now I would be a minority in the West for the rest of my life. But at least I would be left alone, to breathe freely.

The flight from Beijing made a scheduled landing half an hour later in Tianjin. Everybody passed the final passport inspection except me. The inspector examined my passport carefully and said: "We'll have to keep this for a while."

While I waited for its return, every minute felt like an hour. I was nervous. Was this an eleventh-hour hitch? The other passengers were looking at me and growing impatient.

Half-an-hour later, I was given my passport back with no explanation. Had they checked with Beijing to find out whether this brand new passport was authentic? I didn't know, but now it didn't matter.

Not long after the plane took off, I realized the woman seated next to me looked familiar. We had been colleagues in the 1950s. She still worked for the foreign trade corporation and was on her way to New York on business. Thirty years earlier, we had worked in the same building. She had been in the mainstream ever since; I had once tried very hard to be, but never made it.

In the course of conversation, somewhere between China and

Canada, she said: "You're in a better situation than I am."

I was startled. I couldn't imagine what she had in mind. I thought she was in a much more privileged position, able to travel between China and the West and enjoy the pleasures of both worlds.

"What do you mean by that?"

She sighed, and said softly: "You have more freedom to do things . . . your way."

Epilogue

[2007]

Foxspirit was published in Montreal in 1992 by Véhicule Press and won the QSPELL award for non-fiction. Five years later, I returned to China for a long-term work assignment that lasted until I retired in 2002.

I was stationed in Taiyuan, the capital city of Shanxi Province (southwest of Beijing), a window through which I witnessed some of the changes that had occurred in China since my departure. I left a Chinese citizen and returned an expatriate. On the one hand, the Chinese looked at and treated me differently than other Chinese. On the other hand, they still considered me one of them. I felt as though I was juggling the past and the present, alternating between feelings of nostalgia and alienation.

I was astounded by the changes in China as I absorbed the unparalleled economic developments that were dazzling the eyes of locals and foreigners alike, the increasing struggles of the less privileged majority and the rampant corruption that was spreading like a disease.

This prompted me to write another book about my experiences in China as both an insider and outsider there, and in Canada where I also had to juggle feelings of belonging and not belonging. It will be called *Foxdream*, a journey to becoming who I am.

Foxspirit was translated into German and published by Schneekluth in 1997. When I showed the English version to a French publisher in Montreal nine years later, he expressed an immediate interest in it, and a French version entitled *Ma Vie en Rouge* will be published by VLB Éditeur in the fall of 2007.

I never expected to see a Chinese version of the book until a publisher in Beijing approached me in 2003. The possibility of seeing *Foxspirit* published in my mother tongue was exciting and irresistible. Despite some misgivings, a contract was signed with Véhicule Press and I began the translation. I hand delivered the Chinese version to Beijing the following year. It all seemed too good to be true—and it was. Although it was just the story of my life, it did not make it past the Chinese censors. Despite the tremendous changes in China, it appears that some things remain unchanged.

Publisher's Note

After receiving landed immigrant status in August 1986, Zhimei Zhang began the necessary paperwork to bring her children to Canada. Lulu, her youngest, came first in March 1987, followed by Yan in January 1989. On November 17, 1989, Zhimei Zhang became a Canadian citizen.

Zhimei Zhang lives in Montreal where she works as an analyst and administrator for an engineering firm that does business with China.